Soulful Flavors: Unearthing African Culinary Tapestry

Deborah Maria Collier

Published by Collier Deborah Maria, 2024.

SOULFUL FLAVORS: UNEARTHING AFRICAN CULINARY TAPESTRY

First edition. March 27, 2024.

Copyright © 2024 Deborah Maria Collier.

ISBN: 979-8224211814

Written by Deborah Maria Collier.

Table of Contents

Introduction - The definition and importance of culinary heritage in Africa

Culinary heritage refers to the distinctive food traditions and practices that have been passed down through generations within a particular cultural or regional group. It encompasses the recipes, ingredients, cooking techniques, and food customs that are deeply rooted in a community's history and encompass all aspects of food, from cultivation and preparation to serving and consumption.

Culinary heritage plays a significant role in shaping a community's identity and sense of belonging. In Africa, where cultural diversity is abound, culinary heritage holds immense importance, reflecting the continent's history, geography, climate, and cultural dynamics.

One of the most striking aspects of African culinary heritage is its diversity. With over 2,000 distinct ethnic groups and thousands of traditional dishes, Africa showcases an incredible array of culinary traditions. From the Berber cuisine of North Africa to the Ethiopian injera and the South African bobotie, each region and community has its own unique culinary identity.

Africa's culinary heritage is deeply intertwined with its history and cultural practices. Traditional food preparation techniques often involve communal cooking, where multiple generations or members of the community come together to prepare elaborate dishes. These cooking sessions serve as a platform for preserving cultural values, sharing knowledge, and fostering social cohesion.

These traditions also demonstrate a deep relationship between food and nature. African culinary heritage values locally sourced ingredients that are often harvested sustainably and seasonally. This close connection to the land not only emphasizes respect for nature but also promotes healthy and nutritious food practices.

In addition to its cultural and historical significance, culinary heritage in Africa has economic implications. Many African countries are promoting culinary tourism, recognizing that their traditional cuisines can attract visitors from around the world. By showcasing their culinary heritage, African nations and communities are able to boost their local economies and create sustainable livelihoods.

Preserving and celebrating culinary heritage is vital for the continent's cultural conservation and appreciation. As African society experiences rapid modernization and globalization, traditional culinary practices are at risk of being marginalized or replaced by Westernized or industrialized food trends. To prevent this loss, initiatives are being undertaken to document and promote African culinary heritage.

Organizations and individuals are collecting and recording traditional recipes, sharing cooking techniques, and holding culinary workshops and events. This preservation effort helps to create awareness and appreciation for Africa's culinary diversity, reinforcing a sense of pride and identity among the local communities.

In conclusion, culinary heritage in Africa encompasses the rich and diverse food traditions of various ethnic groups. It not only reflects the continent's history and cultural practices but also serves as a means of fostering social cohesion, promoting sustainable practices, and generating economic opportunities. Preserving and valuing the culinary heritage of Africa is crucial to safeguarding its cultural identity and promoting a deeper understanding and appreciation of the continent's diverse communities.

- The challenges and opportunities of preserving culinary heritage in Africa

Preserving culinary heritage in Africa poses both challenges and opportunities due to various factors affecting the continent's food culture. Africa's culinary heritage is rich in flavors, techniques, and ingredients, contributing to its diverse and fascinating food traditions. However, with rapid globalization and societal changes, the preservation of this heritage is becoming increasingly difficult. Here, we will explore the challenges and opportunities involved in maintaining Africa's culinary legacy.

One significant challenge in preserving culinary heritage in Africa stems from the lack of documentation and record-keeping. Traditionally, African culinary traditions have been passed down through generations orally, with little written evidence available. As a result, valuable recipes, techniques, and historical context can be lost over time. It is crucial to find innovative ways to document these culinary traditions, such as partnering with local communities, chefs, and historians to record recipes, cooking processes, and cultural significance.

Another obstacle in preserving culinary heritage is greatly influenced by the impacts of globalization. With the rise of fast food chains and processed foods, traditional African dishes are at risk of being overshadowed by Western cuisines. Younger generations are increasingly opting for convenience and unfamiliar flavors, leading to a decline in traditional food consumption. Educating and raising awareness about the cultural significance and health benefits of traditional African cuisines among younger generations is of utmost importance to combat this trend.

Additionally, changing agricultural practices and environmental challenges have an impact on culinary heritage preservation. The demand for cash crops and monoculture agriculture threatens the biodiversity of traditional African ingredients. Climate change also affects the availability and quality of certain ingredients. Collaborative efforts between culinary professionals, farmers, and environmentalists are necessary to establish sustainable practices and maintain the integrity of culinary heritage.

Despite these challenges, there are numerous opportunities to preserve and elevate Africa's culinary heritage. One opportunity lies in the development of gastronomic tourism. African countries can tap into the growing global interest in food tourism by promoting traditional dishes and culinary experiences. This would not only help generate income for local communities but also raise awareness of the importance of preserving culinary heritage.

Another opportunity lies in the collaboration between chefs, researchers, and food enthusiasts. By working together, they can document, study, and innovate traditional African culinary techniques. This approach can open doors to local and international markets by combining traditional knowledge with contemporary culinary trends.

Furthermore, technology offers unprecedented opportunities to preserve culinary heritage. Online platforms, blogs, and social media can be utilized to share traditional recipes, food stories, and cooking techniques. By embracing digital platforms, African chefs and food enthusiasts can reach broader audiences globally, raising awareness and appreciation for African culinary traditions.

Government support is essential in preserving culinary heritage in Africa. Policies can be implemented to protect local food systems, promote traditional farming practices, and encourage the use of local ingredients in restaurants and homes. Educational initiatives in schools and universities can provide platforms to teach the next generation about their food heritage and its significance.

In conclusion, preserving culinary heritage in Africa comes with its challenges and opportunities. While globalization and changing food preferences pose threats to traditional food cultures, there are also unprecedented opportunities for innovation and collaboration. By valuing, documenting, educating, and embracing technology, the richness of Africa's culinary heritage can endure for generations to come.

- The main themes and objectives of the book

The main themes explored in the book are (1) the impact of colonization and the struggle for independence, (2) the complexities of identity and belonging, (3) the power dynamics between different social classes, (4) the role of religion and spirituality in people's lives, and (5) the search for truth and emotional fulfilment.

Throughout the book, the theme of the impact of colonization is prominently featured. It delves into the grim history of how colonizers imposed their authority and suppressed the native cultures. It explores the psychological and societal aftermath on both the colonized individuals and their communities. The book vividly depicts the atrocities faced by the indigenous peoples, as well as their resistance and fight for freedom.

The complexities of identity and belonging emerge as another significant theme. Characters in the book grapple with their cultural heritage, attempting to navigate between their indigenous roots and the influences of the dominant colonial culture. The exploration of this theme sheds light on the struggles endured by individuals torn between two worlds. It presents a compelling narrative of the search for one's true identity and the challenges faced in asserting that identity in a world shaped by colonization.

The power dynamics between different social classes is also central to the book. It delves into the harsh realities of social hierarchies, where wealth and privilege dictate one's position in society. Through various characters, the book portrays the immense gaps in socioeconomic status and the inequalities faced by the less fortunate. It raises important questions about the morality and ethics of class divisions, showing how class can influence relationships, opportunities, and the overall trajectory of one's life.

Religion and spirituality play a significant role in the narrative. The book explores the different belief systems that coexist and clash within a post-colonial society. It examines the ways in which religious institutions become tools of control and liberation. It delves into the role of spirituality in people's lives, offering solace, guidance, and a sense of purpose. The diverse religious practices and rituals showcased in the book illuminate the complexities of faith and its impact on individual and collective experiences.

Finally, the search for truth and emotional fulfillment emerges as a driving force behind many characters' actions. In a society scarred by colonization, characters embark on journeys to find meaning, fulfillment, and resolution. This search for truth often involves confronting past traumas and breaking free from emotional bondage. The book explores how individuals can strive to heal themselves and their communities, paving the way for personal growth and societal transformation.

The rich and detailed exploration of these themes in the book captivates readers, immersing them in a world that grapples with the repercussions of colonization. The author skillfully weaves these themes together, creating a multi-layered narrative that engages both the intellect and the emotions. With its thought-provoking content and complex characters, the book offers a unique and rewarding reading experience.

Chapter 1: The Origins of African Cuisine-The historical and geographical factors that shaped African cuisine

African cuisine is a rich tapestry of flavors, ingredients, and cooking techniques that have been developed over thousands of years. Its origins can be traced back to a combination of historical and geographical factors that influenced the way food was grown, prepared, and consumed. In this chapter, we will explore these factors and how they have shaped African cuisine into the diverse and vibrant culinary identity it is today.

1. The Beginnings of African Cuisine:

To understand African cuisine, we must delve into the continent's deep history. Fossil evidence suggests that Homo erectus, one of the early human ancestors, inhabited Africa around 1.9 million years ago. As these early humans transitioned from hunter-gatherer societies to settled agricultural communities, their diet underwent significant changes. They started cultivating crops such as sorghum, millet, yams, and lentils, which soon became staples in African cuisine.

2. The Influence of Ancient Civilizations:

Africa boasts a rich history of ancient civilizations, such as Egyptian, Nubian, and Axumite empires. These civilizations revolutionized agriculture by introducing advanced irrigation techniques, animal domestication, and the cultivation of nutritious crops like wheat and barley. The culinary practices of these sophisticated societies, like the use of herbs and spices, cooking methods, and food preservation techniques, laid the foundation for future African cuisines.

3. From the Spice Trade to Trade Routes:

Starting from the 15th century, Europeans began their exploration of Africa, searching for new trade routes and valuable commodities. The arrival of Portuguese, Dutch, and British traders brought spices, fruits, and vegetables from the Far East and South America, thus introducing new ingredients and flavor profiles into African cuisine. This merging of cultures led to the development of unique dishes and cooking styles.

4. The Impact of Slavery and the African Diaspora:

One cannot discuss the origins of African cuisine without acknowledging the tragic history of slave trade and its consequences. The transatlantic slave trade dispersed African people across the globe, taking their culinary traditions with them. Enslaved Africans living in the Americas preserved their food heritage by adapting it to the locally available ingredients. This fusion resulted in iconic dishes like gumbo in the United States or feijoada in Brazil, representing the resilience and creativity of Africans in difficult times.

5. The Environmental Diversity of Africa:

Africa is a vast continent with diverse geographical features such as mountains, deserts, savannahs, rainforests, and valleys. Each region offers a unique array of local ingredients and influences the cuisine found there. For example, along the coasts, seafood plays a prominent role, while inland regions rely more on grains, tubers, and game meat. The availability of specific ingredients and the climate greatly impacted cooking techniques, preservation methods, and flavor profiles.

6. Cultural Diversity and Influences:

The continent itself is home to over 2,000 distinct ethnic groups, each with its own language, customs, and culinary traditions. This cultural diversity has greatly influenced African cuisine, with each region boasting their signature dishes and ingredients. For example, West African cuisine incorporates bold flavors such as peanuts, plantains, and scotch bonnet peppers, while East African cuisine showcases a mix of aromatic herbs, coconut, and seafood.

AFRICAN CUISINE IS a result of centuries of historical and geographical influences that shaped its development and identity. From ancient civilizations to modern-day fusion, the diversity and vibrancy found in African cuisine is a testament to its rich heritage. Understanding the origins of African cuisine allows us to appreciate its complexities, learn from its techniques, and join in celebrating its cultural significance. In the following chapters, we will delve into the specifics of various African cuisines, exploring their unique characteristics and culinary delights.

- The influences and exchanges of African cuisine with other regions

The influences and exchanges of African cuisine with other regions have played a crucial role in shaping the diverse and vibrant culinary practices we see in Africa today. From the early trade routes that connected Africa with the Middle East, to the colonial histories that brought African ingredients and techniques to continents like Europe and the Americas, African cuisine has richly informed and been informed by these interactions.

One of the key influences on African cuisine came through the vast network of trade routes that crisscrossed the African continent. Arabic spice traders brought with them new flavors such as cinnamon, cloves, and black pepper, which melded with the local ingredients and cooking techniques to create unique dishes. The popularity of ingredients like spices, incense, and gold from Africa further facilitated cultural and culinary exchange with regions like the Middle East, India, and beyond. One notable example is the North African dish, couscous, which is thought to have originated in ancient Persia but became an integral part of North African cuisine through the Maghreb trade routes.

European colonialism also had a profound impact on African culinary traditions. As Europeans traversed the continent, they brought with them new ingredients like maize, cassava, and chili peppers, which eventually became staple crops in many African regions. European cooking methods, such as baking and food preservation techniques, also influenced African cooking styles. The fusion of European and African culinary practices resulted in aromatic stews like the Cape Malay curry in South Africa and the fusion cuisine of Senegalese Thiéboudienne, a dish that combines traditional West African flavors with French techniques and ingredients.

Furthermore, African cuisine heavily influenced the local culinary practices of the Americas through the transatlantic slave trade that brought millions of Africans to the New World. These African culinary traditions profoundly influenced Creole cuisine in the Caribbean and West Africa, and Gullah cuisine in the low country of South Carolina and Georgia. Ingredients such as okra, yams, black-eyed peas, and collard greens became integral parts of the local food culture, along with cooking methods such as slow cooking and stewing.

Moreover, the African diaspora in the Americas also led to the emergence of cultural hubs where African and local cuisines blended to create vibrant culinary traditions. In cities like Bahia in Brazil, New Orleans in the United States, and Port-au-Prince in Haiti, African flavors played an essential role in creating iconic dishes such as Acarajé, Gumbo, and Griot.

Today, the influences and exchanges of African cuisine continue to shape global food trends. With the rise of the African diaspora, African ingredients, spices, and dishes are finding their place in mainstream culinary scenes worldwide. African food festivals, fusion restaurants, and vibrant cookbooks are testaments to the increasing recognition of African flavors and cooking techniques.

In conclusion, the influences and exchanges of African cuisine with other regions have contributed significantly to the diverse and dynamic culinary landscape we observe today. From the trading routes of the past to the colonial interactions and the African diaspora, these exchanges have enriched and expanded African cuisine in ways that continue to shape world gastronomy.

- The examples and recipes of dishes that reflect the origins of African cuisine

African cuisine is incredibly diverse, with each region in the continent offering a unique array of flavors, ingredients, and cooking techniques. From the rich stews of West Africa to the spicy curries of East Africa, the dishes that have evolved from African heritage are a true reflection of the continent's history and culture. In this article, we will explore a few fascinating examples and recipes of dishes that showcase the origins of African cuisine.

1. Jollof Rice (West Africa):

Jollof rice is a popular dish in many West African countries, including Nigeria, Ghana, and Senegal. It originates from the Wolof people of Senegal and Gambia. This flavorsome and vibrant one-pot rice dish is cooked with tomatoes, onions, red bell peppers, and various spices. It often includes protein sources like chicken, beef, or fish, making it a hearty and satisfying meal. Jollof rice represents the diverse culinary heritage of West Africa, with each country or region adding its own twist.

2. Bobotie (South Africa):

Bobotie is a traditional South African dish with its roots in Cape Malay cuisine. It is a baked casserole dish made with minced meat, usually beef or lamb, combined with aromatic spices such as curry powder, turmeric, and ginger. The meat mixture is topped with a custard-like egg topping and baked until golden brown. Bobotie showcases the fusion of African and Asian flavors brought by the Malay slaves who were brought to South Africa by Dutch settlers. It is often served with yellow rice, chutney, and sambal.

3. Injera (Ethiopia):

Injera is a sourdough flatbread that is a staple in Ethiopian and Eritrean cuisine. Made from fermented teff, a tiny grain indigenous to the region, it is cooked on large circular griddles and has a slightly sour flavor. Injera is not only a versatile bread used as a utensil for scooping up various dishes but also a significant part of Ethiopia's cultural identity. It reflects the rich agricultural heritage of the area and is often accompanied by a variety of stews and sautéed vegetables.

4. Moambe Chicken (Central Africa):

Moambe chicken, also known as poulet moambe, is a popular dish in Central Africa, particularly in the Democratic Republic of Congo. This flavorful chicken dish consists of chicken cooked in a sauce made from moambe, or red palm fruit paste. The sauce is spiced with garlic, onions, and black pepper, which adds depth and heat to the dish. Moambe chicken is typically served with fufu or rice, and it reflects the abundant use of regional ingredients found in Central Africa.

5. Bunny Chow (South Africa):

Originating from Durban, South Africa, bunny chow is a popular street food dish. It consists of a hollowed-out loaf of bread filled with flavorful curry. The curry can be vegetarian, chicken, lamb, or beef, and it is typically quite spicy. Bunny chow is a delicious fusion of Indian flavors, brought to South Africa during the indentured laborer era, combined with local ingredients and preferences. It represents the intriguing culinary connections between South Africa and the Indian subcontinent.

These examples and recipes offer just a small glimpse into the vast world of African cuisine. Each dish reflects the diverse origins, history, and culture of the regions they hail from. Exploring the culinary heritage of Africa through its delightful and authentic dishes is an adventure that unveils the richness of the continent's food traditions.

Chapter 2: The Diversity of African Cuisine- The overview and characteristics of African cuisine

African cuisine is often perceived as a monolithic entity, with stereotypes and misconceptions clouding its true diversity and richness. In reality, Africa is a vast continent that is home to 54 countries, each with its own distinctive culinary traditions and flavors. In this chapter, we delve into the fascinating world of African cuisine, unraveling its regional and cultural variations, while highlighting the shared characteristics that unite this diverse culinary landscape.

Regional Variations:

One cannot consider African cuisine as a single entity without recognizing the diverse regional variations that exist across the continent. From the spice-infused dishes of North Africa to the vibrant flavors of West Africa and the savory stews of Southern Africa, each region boasts a culinary heritage that is deeply rooted in its history, climate, and geographical influences.

North African Cuisine:

North African cuisine is heavily influenced by the Arab, Berber, and Ottoman culinary traditions. With dishes like couscous, tagines, and harissa, the flavors often bear a strong Mediterranean influence. Ingredients such as olive oil, cumin, and coriander are commonly used in North African cuisine, giving it a distinct flavor profile that is both aromatic and complex.

West African Cuisine:

West African cuisine is renowned for its bold flavors and use of various spices. From jollof rice, a flavorful one-pot dish, to the ubiquitously beloved suya, a grilled meat skewer seasoned with a mixture of spices, West African cuisine is a true testament to the rich heritage of the African diaspora. Peanuts, yams, plantains, and okra are staple ingredients in this region, which contribute to the unique taste and texture of its dishes.

East African Cuisine:

The cuisine of East Africa reflects strong Indian, Arabic, and Portuguese influences due to historical trade routes. With dishes like injera, a spongy fermented bread, and pilau rice, East African cuisine demonstrates the richness of aromatic spices like cardamom, cinnamon, and cloves. Additionally, the coastal regions of East Africa thrive on an abundance of seafood, resulting in deliciously flavorful dishes such as Zanzibar's famous coconut-based curries.

Southern African Cuisine:

Southern African cuisine is distinctively different from the rest of Africa, largely due to the region's historical British and Dutch influences. Braai, a type of barbecued meat, is a truly South African tradition that brings people together. The popular addition of chutneys, fruit preserves, and peri-peri sauces further enhance the flavors of the grilled dishes. The region also embraces wild game meat, such as ostrich, springbok, and warthog, adding a unique touch to their culinary repertoire.

Shared Characteristics:

While the regional variations are undoubtedly striking, African cuisine also exhibits shared characteristics that serve as threads stitching the continent's diverse culinary fabric together.

Fresh Ingredients and Local Produce:

African cuisine heavily relies on locally sourced, fresh ingredients. From leafy greens like sorrel and amaranth to tropical fruits like mangoes and jackfruits, African dishes celebrate the abundant flavors of the continent. The rich biodiversity and fertile soils of Africa contribute significantly to the freshness and diversity of its ingredients.

One-Pot Wonders:

Many African dishes are characterized by their delicious one-pot cooking style. Dishes like jollof rice, bobotie, and tagines are prepared by combining various ingredients in a single pot, allowing the flavors to meld and create a harmonious combination that delights the taste buds. This method of cooking not only simplifies meal preparation but also ensures that every bite is a sensory experience.

Diverse Use of Indigenous Grains and Legumes:

Throughout Africa, indigenous grains and legumes are integral components of the diverse cuisine. Sorghum, millet, and teff are popular grains used in dishes like couscous, injera, and porridges. Additionally, the use of legumes such as black-eyed peas, cowpeas, and lentils adds nutritional value and complexity to many African dishes.

AFRICAN CUISINE IS an exploration of flavors, traditions, and cultural influences that encapsulate the continent's diversity. From the aromatic tagines of North Africa to the fiery flavors of West Africa, and the hearty stews of Southern Africa, African cuisine reflects a vibrant tapestry of tastes and culinary artistry. By embracing the shared characteristics and celebrating the regional variations, one can better appreciate and understand the depth and sophistication of African gastronomy.

- The regional and national variations of African cuisine

African cuisine is as diverse as the continent itself. From the spicy flavors of North Africa to the hearty dishes of West Africa and the delectable seafood in the coastal regions, each region within Africa has its unique culinary traditions and flavors.

In North Africa, Moroccan, Tunisian, and Algerian cuisine are popular and well-known for their spicy and flavorful dishes. Traditional dishes like tagines, couscous, and harissa are common in restaurants and homes. These countries are heavily influenced by Mediterranean flavors and have a rich combination of herbs and spices such as cumin, coriander, saffron, and ginger. Moroccan cuisine often features slow-cooked meat with dried fruits and aromatic spices, giving dishes a sweet and savory taste.

Moving towards West Africa, one will encounter a variety of bold and flavorful dishes. Countries like Nigeria, Senegal, and Ghana have a wide range of dishes that use local ingredients including vegetables, grains, and tropical fruits. Nigerian cuisine is known for its delicious stews, such as egusi soup and jollof rice, while Senegal is renowned for vibrant dishes like yassa chicken and thieboudienne, a tantalizing fish and rice dish. Rich soups made from yam, cassava, or pumpkin leaves are also prevalent in this region.

Heading towards East Africa, one will find a contrasting array of flavors. Ethiopia takes the spotlight with its distinctive and diverse cuisine. Ethiopian dishes are unique due to the use of a fermented bread called injera. This sourdough flatbread acts as both a staple and a utensil. Spicy stews made from various meats, lentils, and vegetables called wats are often served on top of the injera. The vibrant and aromatic spices like berbere, a hot pepper-based spice mix, are what make Ethiopian cuisine stand out.

Coastal regions of Africa, such as South Africa, Kenya, and Tanzania, are known for their abundant seafood dishes due to their proximity to the ocean. Grilled, baked, or stewed fish and shellfish form a significant part of the diet in these regions. Popular dishes in South Africa include sosaties, which are skewered meats marinated in a sweet and savory sauce, and bobotie, a flavorful and hearty baked mince dish. Kenyan and Tanzanian cuisine feature a blend of Indian, Arabic, and East African flavors with dishes like pilau, biryani, and samosas being widely savored.

Each region of Africa has its distinct cooking techniques, flavors, and ingredients that reflect the rich history and culture of the area. Spices, such as cloves, cardamom, and allspice, are commonly used in East Africa while peanuts, beans, and root vegetables are recurring elements in West African cuisine. The use of ingredients like tamarind, coconut milk, and palm oil are prevalent in coastal regions.

National and regional variations within African cuisine offer a culinary adventure like no other. With its diverse flavors, spices, and cooking techniques, African cuisine is a delicious exploration of the continent's cultural heritage and culinary legacy. Whether it's the fiery flavors of North Africa or the bold and vibrant dishes of West Africa, African cuisine is a feast for the senses that will surely leave you craving for more.

- The examples and recipes of dishes that reflect the diversity of African cuisine

African cuisine is incredibly diverse, with each region offering its unique flavors and cooking techniques. From spicy stews to savory rice dishes and flavorful grilled meats, the examples and recipes of African dishes truly showcase the richness and variety of the continent's culinary traditions.

One classic example of African cuisine is Jollof Rice, which is beloved in West Africa, particularly in Nigeria and Ghana. Jollof Rice is a one-pot dish made with rice, tomatoes, onions, and a variety of spices such as garlic, ginger, and chili flakes. The dish gets its vibrant red color from the tomatoes and is often cooked with chicken or beef for added flavor. Jollof Rice is not only delicious but also culturally significant, often a centerpiece at celebrations and family gatherings.

Moving to East Africa, we find a variety of aromatic stews and vegetable dishes that are staples in the region's cuisine. One popular dish is Ethiopian Doro Wat, a spicy chicken stew served with injera, a traditional sourdough flatbread. Doro Wat features a rich blend of spices such as berbere (a fiery spice mixture), paprika, and ginger. It is slow-cooked with onions, garlic, and chicken drumsticks until the flavors meld together to create a hearty and flavorful dish.

South Africa has its unique contribution to the African culinary scene with the beloved dish known as Bobotie. Bobotie is a traditional Cape Malay dish consisting of spiced minced meat (generally beef or lamb) topped with an egg-based custard. The filling is made with a mix of onions, garlic, ginger, curry powder, and fruit chutney, giving it a savory-sweet flavor profile. It is then baked in the oven until the custard sets and forms a golden-brown crust. Bobotie is often served with yellow rice and a variety of sides like pickles, coconut, and sliced bananas to add contrasting flavors and textures.

Morocco, a North African country, is known for its aromatic tagines, which are slow-cooked stews prepared in a distinctive conical-shaped clay pot known as a tagine. One example is the Tagine with Chicken and Preserved Lemons, a dish made with spices like cumin, cinnamon, and paprika. It also combines flavors like olives, saffron, and preserved lemons to create a savory and tangy flavor profile. The chicken is tender and incredibly aromatic, making it a staple dish in Moroccan households.

In conclusion, African cuisine is brimming with a myriad of dishes that reflect the continent's rich cultural tapestry. From the flavorful Jollof Rice in West Africa to the aromatic Ethiopian Doro Wat in East Africa, the hearty Bobotie in South Africa, and the fragrant Tagine with Chicken and Preserved Lemons in North Africa, African cuisine showcases a diverse range of tastes, flavors, and cooking techniques. Exploring these examples and trying out the recipes allows one to truly appreciate the depth and variety of African culinary traditions.

Chapter 3: The Rituals of African Cuisine-The significance and purpose of rituals in African cuisine

African cuisine is not merely about the flavors and ingredients; it is a rich tapestry of cultural practices and beliefs that are deeply intertwined with everyday life. One essential aspect of African culinary traditions is the presence of rituals. These rituals serve a significant purpose in African cuisine, going beyond the act of eating and cooking. In this chapter, we will delve into the significance and purpose of rituals in African cuisine, exploring how they shape culinary practices, enhance social cohesion, and transmit cultural knowledge down through generations.

Rituals and Cultural Significance:

Rituals hold immense cultural importance in African cuisine, acting as containers of community knowledge and ancestral wisdom. They are deeply rooted in historical, spiritual, and social contexts, and their performance is considered necessary for maintaining harmony and balance within African societies. These rituals are multifaceted, encompassing various aspects such as food preparation, communal eating, and offering gratitude to ancestral spirits. Understanding the cultural significance of these rituals reveals a deep insight into the history, values, and beliefs of African cultures.

Enhancing Social Cohesion:

One of the key objectives of food-related rituals in African cuisine is to strengthen social bonds and create a sense of togetherness within the community. Food is a unifying force, and communal meals serve as the heart of African societies. Through the shared experience of food preparation, serving, and consumption, rituals forge connections between individuals, families, and communities. They provide a platform for storytelling, knowledge transmission, and fostering a sense of identity and belonging.

Transmitting Cultural Knowledge:

African cuisine is an embodiment of cultural heritage, and rituals play a fundamental role in preserving and transmitting this knowledge from one generation to the next. Elders and experienced cooks are entrusted with the responsibility of passing down traditional cooking techniques, secret recipes, and cultural values through the performance of rituals. By actively involving younger members, these rituals ensure the continuity and preservation of culinary traditions, keeping African cultural identities alive.

Harnessing Spiritual Dimensions:

Rituals in African cuisine often possess strong spiritual dimensions, intertwining the physical act of preparing and consuming food with the sacred. The offering of food and libations to ancestral spirits, deities, or divine forces is a common ritualistic practice in African cultures. This act acknowledges the role of spiritual entities in the success and well-being of the community, fostering a reciprocal relationship based on respect and gratitude. These spiritual dimensions add depth and meaning to food rituals, deeply connecting African communities to their religious and cultural beliefs.

IN CONCLUSION, THE rituals found within African cuisine serve as powerful vessels of cultural knowledge, enhance social cohesion, and give meaning to culinary practices. They go beyond the realm of food and nourishment, encapsulating the rich history, values, and beliefs of African societies. Understanding the significance and purpose of these rituals not only provides insight into African culture but also paves the way for the preservation and appreciation of this diverse culinary heritage.

- The types and occasions of rituals in African cuisine

African cuisine is rich in traditions and cultural significance, with rituals playing a crucial role in various aspects of daily life. From birth to marriage, and even in times of mourning, certain types of rituals and their corresponding occasions are deeply ingrained in African culture.

One of the most common types of rituals in African cuisine is the gathering ritual, which involves individuals coming together for a specific purpose, often revolving around food. This type of ritual is prevalent in many African communities and is used to celebrate important events or milestones. Whether it is a wedding ceremony, a birth celebration, or a harvest festival, the gathering ritual brings people together to indulge in the delights of African cuisine.

Another type of ritual in African cuisine is the initiation or rite of passage ritual. This type of ritual marks significant life transitions, such as reaching puberty or becoming a full-fledged member of a community. Often accompanied by specific food-related customs and ceremonies, initiation rituals play a fundamental role in African culture. For example, young individuals in certain African tribes may go through elaborate ceremonies involving a special diet, symbolic meals, and communal feasting to mark their transition into adulthood.

Furthermore, ancestor rituals are an integral part of African cuisine and occur during moments of remembrance and reverence for ancestors. These rituals are deeply rooted in a belief system that emphasizes the spiritual connection between the living and the deceased. African communities engage in various activities to honor their ancestors, such as pouring libations, sacrificing animals, and preparing traditional dishes as offerings. These rituals aim to maintain a strong connection with one's ancestors and to seek their guidance and blessings in daily life.

In some African cultures, healing rituals are practiced to address health-related issues and imbalances within the community. Traditional healers or medicine men and women play a vital role in these rituals, utilizing a combination of herbal remedies, rituals, and specific diets. The underlying belief during these rituals is that food can be used as a means to restore physical and spiritual well-being, promoting healing and balance within individuals and the community.

Lastly, mourning rituals hold great importance in African cuisine, serving as a way to support grieving families and honor the deceased. These rituals usually involve the preparation and sharing of meals, symbolizing communal support and solidarity with those in mourning. Certain dishes may be prepared specifically for mourning occasions, and community members often come together to provide nourishment and comfort during these difficult times.

In conclusion, the types and occasions of rituals in African cuisine are diverse and intricately interwoven into the fabric of African culture. Gathering rituals, initiation rituals, ancestor rituals, healing rituals, and mourning rituals all serve to foster unity, preserve traditions, and celebrate significant moments in African communities. These rituals are not only about the food itself but also about the connections, beliefs, and values that are shared among individuals.

- The examples and recipes of dishes that reflect the rituals of African cuisine

African cuisine is known for its rich flavors, vibrant colors, and use of unique ingredients. But food in Africa is not just about nourishment, it is deeply rooted in cultural traditions and rituals that have been passed down for generations. Today, we will explore some examples and recipes of dishes that reflect the rituals of African cuisine.

One classic dish that is often prepared during special occasions is Jollof Rice. This dish, which originated in West Africa, is a symbol of sharing and coming together as a community. It is usually cooked in a single pot and is a staple at weddings, family gatherings, and celebratory events.

To make Jollof Rice, you will need the following ingredients:

- 2 cups of long-grain rice
- 1 onion, finely chopped
- 2 cloves of garlic, minced
- 2 tomatoes, blended
- 1 red bell pepper, blended
- 1 teaspoon of thyme
- 1 teaspoon of paprika
- 1 teaspoon of curry powder
- Salt and pepper to taste
- 2 cups of chicken or vegetable broth
- 2 tablespoons of vegetable oil

Start by rinsing the rice thoroughly and set it aside. In a large pot, heat the vegetable oil over medium heat. Add the chopped onions and garlic and sauté until they turn translucent. Next, add the blended tomatoes and bell pepper and cook for about five minutes, stirring occasionally.

Now, it's time to add the spices. Add the thyme, paprika, curry powder, salt, and pepper to the pot. Stir well to coat the vegetables with the spices. Then, add the rice and stir until it is well combined with the tomato mixture.

Finally, pour in the chicken or vegetable broth and bring the mixture to a boil. Reduce the heat to low, cover the pot, and let the rice simmer for about 20-25 minutes, or until the rice is cooked through and all the liquid is absorbed.

Jollof Rice is typically served with grilled or fried chicken, roasted plantains, or a side salad. It is a dish that brings people together, as it is often shared among family and friends.

Another example of a dish that reflects the rituals of African cuisine is Injera, a spongy sourdough flatbread that is a staple in Ethiopian and Eritrean cuisine. Injera is not only a delicious accompaniment to stews and curries but it is also an essential part of communal eating traditions.

To make Injera, you will need the following ingredients:
- 2 cups of teff flour (or a combination of teff and all-purpose flour)
- 3 cups of water
- 1 teaspoon of active dry yeast
- Salt to taste

In a large mixing bowl, combine the teff flour (or teff and all-purpose flour mixture) with water and stir until well mixed. Add the yeast and salt and whisk until the batter is smooth and without lumps. Cover the bowl with a clean kitchen towel and let it sit at room temperature for at least 12 hours.

After fermentation, the batter will be slightly bubbly and have a tangy aroma. To cook the Injera, you will need a large non-stick skillet or a traditional Ethiopian clay pan called a mitad.

Heat the skillet over medium-high heat and lightly grease it with oil. Pour a ladleful of the batter onto the pan, swirling it around to create a thin, pancake-like layer. Cook the Injera for about 2-3 minutes until holes form on the surface and the edges start to curl up.

Gently remove the Injera from the pan and repeat the process with the remaining batter. Traditionally, Injera is served as a base for various stews and curries, such as Doro Wat (a spiced chicken stew) or Misir Wat (a lentil stew).

In African cuisine, these examples and countless other dishes not only showcase the rich culinary heritage but also reflect the significant cultural rituals and values. From communal feasting to the use of local ingredients, African cuisine is deeply intertwined with tradition and continues to bring people together through food.

Chapter 4: The Stories of African Cuisine- The role and function of stories in African cuisine

4.1 In this chapter, we will delve into the fascinating world of African cuisine, exploring the role and function of stories within this culinary tradition. Stories in African cuisine serve a unique purpose, holding cultural, historical, and social significance. They provide a rich tapestry of narratives, passed down through generations, which shape the culinary practices of diverse African communities. This chapter will explore various types of stories associated with African cuisine and discuss how they contribute to the preservation and evolution of this vibrant culinary heritage.

4.2 Origins of African Cuisine Stories

African cuisine stories draw inspiration from various sources, including mythical tales, folklore, ancestral wisdom, and the oral tradition. These stories not only transmit knowledge about the preparation and consumption of food but also reflect the cultural values, religious beliefs, and social customs of African communities. They paint vivid pictures of ancient times, outline traditional cooking techniques, and emphasize the importance of communal dining.

4.2.1 Mythical Tales

Mythical tales hold a significant place in African cuisine stories. They explain the origins of ingredients, cooking utensils, and culinary practices. These stories often feature supernatural beings or deities who teach humans how to cultivate crops, hunt, or prepare traditional dishes. Through these tales, African communities pass down essential skills and knowledge, reinforcing their connection with the land and the food it provides.

4.2.2 Folklore

Folklore stories in African cuisine provide cultural context, reflecting the beliefs, values, and customs of specific regions or tribes. These stories often revolve around culinary rituals and taboos, guiding people's behavior around food. Folklore stories might caution against disrespecting ingredients or provide instructions on proper offerings to spirits when preparing certain dishes. By telling and retelling these tales, African communities reinforce social norms surrounding food.

4.2.3 Ancestral Wisdom

Ancestral wisdom stories highlight the importance of lineage and ancestral connections in African cuisine. These stories convey recipes, techniques, and ingredients that have been passed down from generation to generation, emphasizing the significance of preserving traditional culinary practices. They serve as a tool for keeping ancestral knowledge alive and ensuring the transmission of culinary heritage to future generations.

4.3 The Function of Stories in African Cuisine

Stories in African cuisine serve various functions, all contributing to the richness and depth of this culinary tradition. Let us explore some of these functions in detail.

4.3.1 Cultural Preservation

African cuisine stories play a crucial role in preserving the cultural identity of diverse African communities. By passing down stories that recount the origins and values associated with traditional dishes, communities ensure the sustainable preservation of their culinary heritage. These stories provide a sense of continuity and connection to ancestral traditions, strengthening cultural pride and fostering a deep sense of belonging.

4.3.2 Education and Transmission of Knowledge

Stories in African cuisine act as a source of knowledge, teaching future generations about the art of cooking and dining. They communicate culinary skills, techniques, and recipes, preserving the wisdom gained from centuries of trial and error. By sharing these stories, African communities ensure that their culinary practices are not lost to the forces of globalization and modernization.

4.3.3 Social Bonding

Through stories, African cuisine creates a sense of community and reinforces social bonds. Culinary narratives often revolve around communal cooking, feasting, and celebrations. By sharing stories about their food traditions, African communities strengthen their shared identities and foster a sense of togetherness, uniting people through the experience of shared meals and storytelling.

4.3.4 Connection with the Natural World

African cuisine stories emphasize the connection between people and the natural world. They highlight the importance of respecting the land, understanding seasonal rhythms, and living in harmony with nature. By weaving these stories into their culinary practices, African communities develop a profound reverence for the ingredients they use, fostering sustainable and environmentally conscious approaches to food production and consumption.

4.4 Conclusion

Stories play a vital role in African cuisine, serving as a powerful agent for cultural transmission, education, social bonding, and connection to the natural world. These narratives reflect the intricate tapestry of African culinary traditions, preserving culinary wisdom and ancestral heritage. By recognizing and appreciating the role and function of stories in African cuisine, we can gain a deeper understanding of the significance of this unique culinary heritage and contribute to its preservation and evolution.

- The sources and forms of stories in African cuisine

African cuisine is rich and diverse, with each region having its own unique flavors and culinary traditions. Influenced by the continent's diverse geography and history, African cuisine tells a captivating story through its sources and forms of storytelling. These stories are deeply intertwined within the ingredients, cooking techniques, and cultural significance of the dishes.

One of the primary sources of stories in African cuisine is oral tradition. Throughout Africa, storytelling has been a way of passing down knowledge and preserving cultural heritage for generations. These stories often find expressions in various cooking methods, ingredients, and the overall preparation of food.

For instance, in West Africa, the art of jollof rice tells the story of a hearty and communal tradition of cooking. This beloved dish, which consists of rice cooked in a flavorful tomato-based sauce, often accompanied by a variety of meats, vegetables, and spices, has different variations across the region. Each variation of jollof rice embodies the cultural diversity and historical influences of the people who prepare and enjoy it.

In Eastern Africa, the art of spicing plays a significant role in storytelling through cuisine. Influenced by Indian, Arab, and Persian merchants, the use of spices like ginger, cardamom, coriander, and cumin in dishes such as pilau rice or biryanis showcase the historical trade connections and the fusion of culinary practices in the region.

Another fascinating form of storytelling in African cuisine is through the use of symbolic ingredients. Certain ingredients hold cultural and spiritual meanings, adding depth to the culinary experience. For example, the calabash, a versatile fruit with hard shell and watery flesh, is not only used for serving food but also carries symbolic significance in many African cultures. It represents fertility, abundance, and hospitality, reflecting the values and traditions of the communities it is incorporated into.

Traditional African recipes often invoke symbolic associations to connect people with their cultural heritage. The use of palm oil, a staple in many traditional Nigerian dishes, holds great cultural significance. For many Nigerians, palm oil is not just another cooking ingredient but a representation of prosperity, health, and familial bonds. It is used in dishes such as Egusi soup, which tells a story of sustainability and kinship through its use of local ingredients and cooking techniques.

Furthermore, the preparation and sharing of meals themselves form a powerful narrative in African cuisine. Many traditional African dishes, such as Ethiopian injera or Congolese fufu, are meant to be shared and eaten communally. This act of sharing food not only symbolizes unity and togetherness but also narrates the importance of community and harmonious relationships within African cultures.

The sources and forms of stories in African cuisine are indeed diverse and multi-dimensional. They not only provide a platform to celebrate the rich history and cultural diversity of Africa but also allow individuals to connect with their roots in a meaningful and flavorful way. From the oral traditions preserved in cooking methods to the symbolic ingredients representing cultural values, African cuisine serves as a captivating storyteller, sharing the unique narratives of the continent through the art of food.

- The examples and recipes of dishes that reflect the stories of African cuisine

African cuisine is rich in flavors, colors, and stories that have been passed down through generations. From spicy stews to colorful salads, every dish tells a tale of the people and their culture. In this article, we will explore some examples and recipes of dishes that reflect the stories of African cuisine.

One dish that perfectly embodies the spirit of African cuisine is Jollof rice. This vibrant and flavorful rice dish is popular in West Africa and is often considered the region's staple food. Its origins can be traced back to the Wolof people of Senegal and Gambia, but it has since become a beloved dish across the continent.

Jollof rice is not just a simple rice dish; it is a celebration of African spices and a testament to the creativity of African cooks. The rice is cooked in a tomato-based sauce with a variety of vegetables and spices such as onions, garlic, ginger, and a special blend of spices called "Jollof spice." Some variations also include proteins like chicken, beef, or fish. When the dish is prepared, the rice takes on a vibrant red color due to the tomato sauce, and each bite bursts with bold flavors.

Another dish that reflects the stories of African cuisine is the Ethiopian injera. Injera is a type of sourdough flatbread made from teff flour, a gluten-free grain native to Ethiopia. The preparation of injera involves a fermentation process that gives it a unique, tangy flavor. Traditionally, injera is served on a large platter with various stews and dishes placed on top. Diners tear pieces of the injera and use it to scoop up the stews, creating a communal eating experience.

Injera not only reflects the distinctive flavors of Ethiopian cuisine but also symbolizes the cultural significance of communal dining in African societies. The act of sharing a meal on a large platter and tearing the injera with one's hands fosters a sense of community and togetherness, a value deeply ingrained in African culture.

Moving on to North Africa, the Moroccan tagine is an iconic dish that reflects the diverse histories and cultural influences of the region. A tagine is both a cooking vessel and the name of a slow-cooked stew cooked in that vessel. Its unique conical shape traps steam, allowing the ingredients to cook slowly and develop intense flavors.

Moroccan tagines often feature a combination of ingredients like meat or poultry, vegetables, fruits, and a blend of aromatic spices such as cumin, cinnamon, turmeric, and saffron. The combination of sweet and savory flavors in a tagine mirrors the complexity and diversity of North African culinary traditions. It also highlights the intricate blending of flavors that characterizes African cuisine as a whole.

These examples are just a glimpse into the vast array of dishes that reflect the stories of African cuisine. Each recipe carries with it a narrative that speaks to the diverse cultures, histories, and flavors found across the continent. Through these dishes, we can savor not only the delicious flavors but also the rich heritage and richness of African culinary traditions.

Chapter 5: The Symbols of African Cuisine- The meaning and value of symbols in African cuisine

Symbols play a significant role in African cuisine, offering a gateway to understanding the deep-rooted meanings and cultural values associated with food. In this chapter, we delve into the fascinating world of symbols in African cuisine, exploring the rich and diverse tapestry of meanings held within various culinary practices across the continent. By unraveling these symbols, we can grasp a better understanding of the historical, social, and spiritual significance of African culinary traditions.

Symbolism in Ingredients:

In African cuisine, ingredients hold powerful symbolic meanings that extend beyond their culinary usage. For instance, yams symbolize fertility and abundance in many cultures. The shape and color of vegetables and fruits, such as the roundness of cocoyams or the bright yellow of mangoes, can represent different concepts, from unity to prosperity. These symbols intertwine with traditional beliefs and practices, creating a harmonious relationship between African communities and their food.

The Ritualistic Preparations:

African cuisine is often prepared with meticulous attention to detail, infused with ancient rituals that heighten its symbolic value. The way food is harvested, processed, and cooked represents a sacred bond between mankind, nature, and the spiritual realms. Utensils, such as traditional clay pots, wooden mortars and pestles, have symbolic connections to ancestral traditions, symbolizing veneration and ancestral respect.

Plating and Presentation:

The presentation of African cuisine is a visual art form that speaks to its symbolic significance. Elaborate patterns, colorful arrangements, and the use of natural elements, such as leaves and flowers, contribute to creating visually stunning culinary experiences. Different plating designs reflect cultural identities and convey messages of celebration, prosperity, or even healing.

The Social and Cultural Significance:

Beyond the aesthetic appeal, symbols in African cuisine serve as cultural markers, accentuating social hierarchies, alliances, and rituals. For instance, communal meals and feasts reflect ideas of community cohesion and solidarity. Special dishes and ingredients associated with festivals and celebrations contribute to collective memory and reinforce cultural identity.

Symbolism in Traditional Dishes:

Some African dishes embody profound historical and spiritual meanings within their preparation and consumption. For example, dishes like Jollof rice, fufu, and injera signify unity, strength, and cultural resilience. Certain spices and herbs used in cooking, such as cloves and basil, can be linked to traditional healing practices and can impart a sense of wellness, purifying mind, body, and spirit with every bite.

The Power of Sacred Symbols:

Throughout African culinary traditions, certain sacred symbols hold immense power and are revered by practitioners. These symbols often represent deities, invoke protection, and establish connections between the physical and spiritual worlds. An example is the use of cowrie shells in Nigerian cuisine, which represent prosperity, beauty, and wealth, and can be found in dishes like Egusi soup or pounded yam.

SYMBOLS IN AFRICAN cuisine possess a multifaceted significance, serving as a window into the cultural, historical, and spiritual dimensions of the continent's culinary traditions. From ingredients to preparations, plating to consumption, symbols permeate every aspect, providing individuals with a deeper understanding of their cultural heritage and reinforcing traditions passed down through generations. As we recognize the importance of these symbols, we can foster a greater appreciation for African cuisine, its symbolism, and the narratives it embodies.

- The categories and examples of symbols in African cuisine

In African cuisine, various symbols are utilized to convey specific meanings, enhance the presentation, and perform cultural functions. These symbols can be seen in the choice of ingredients, culinary techniques, food presentation, and even in the rituals associated with certain dishes. Here, we will explore the categories and examples of symbols commonly found in African cuisine.

1. Ingredients as Symbols:

Africans have a strong connection to their land and environment, which is often reflected in the use of certain ingredients as symbols in their cuisine. For instance, the use of yam in West African cooking symbolizes fertility, abundance, and luck. In some cultures, the kola nut is deeply symbolic and usually shared as a sign of hospitality and peace. Another example is the calabash gourd, often used as a symbol of family unity and community.

2. Colors as Symbols:

Colors play a significant role in African cuisine symbolism. Different colors are associated with various meanings and cultural values. Red, for example, is frequently used to symbolize strength, passion, and vitality, which can be seen in dishes like Nigerian jollof rice. Yellow represents wealth, prosperity, and royalty and is often associated with dishes like Ghanaian fufu with palm soup. White symbolizes purity, spirituality, and ancestral connections, as reflected in South African dishes like milk tart.

3. Presentation as Symbols:

African cuisine places great emphasis on visually appealing presentation, using various techniques to create symbolic representations. A popular example is the use of intricate food designs, like those seen in Ethiopian injera bread. The artwork created on the surface of the bread symbolizes unity, harmony, and the communal aspect of meal-sharing. Similarly, the spiral shape of Nigerian banga soup signifies the cyclical and interconnected nature of life.

4. Rituals and Ceremonies as Symbols:

African cuisine often plays a significant role in traditional rituals and ceremonies, acting as a symbol of cultural heritage and spirituality. For example, the preparation and sharing of food during weddings symbolize family bonding and symbolically unifies the couple as they partake in their first communal meal together. In certain rituals, the act of offering food to ancestors symbolizes respect, honor, and the continuity of family traditions.

5. Utensils and Cooking Methods as Symbols:

The utensils and cooking methods used in African cuisine also hold symbolic meanings. For example, the mortar and pestle, used in various African countries, symbolizes hard work, perseverance, and community strength. Cooking techniques such as baking over an open fire, common in many African regions, symbolize the connection to ancestral ways of cooking and the preservation of cultural traditions.

Overall, the symbols found in African cuisine tell rich stories of cultural values, spirituality, unity, and heritage. They reflect the intricate relationship between food, society, and the natural environment. Exploring these symbols not only enhances our understanding of the culinary traditions but also provides insights into the deep-rooted cultural significance present in African cuisine.

- The examples and recipes of dishes that reflect the symbols of African cuisine

African cuisine is rich in flavors, colors, and cultural symbolism. Many dishes are not only a delicious combination of ingredients but also a reflection of the African heritage, history, and beliefs. Let's dive into some examples and delectable recipes that represent the symbols of African cuisine.

1. Jollof Rice (Nigeria/Ghana/Senegal):

Jollof rice is a staple dish in many West African countries, each with its unique variation. The dish is known for its vibrant red color, symbolizing the strength and resilience of the African people. The combination of rice, tomato sauce, onions, and various spices creates a flavorful and satisfying meal. Jollof rice is often served with grilled chicken or fish, making it a complete and fulfilling dish.

Ingredients:

- 2 cups of long-grain rice
- 2 onions, finely chopped
- 4 tomatoes, blended into a puree
- 2 red bell peppers, blended into a puree
- 2 cloves of garlic, minced
- 2 teaspoons of curry powder
- 1 teaspoon of thyme
- 1 teaspoon of paprika
- 1 teaspoon of chili powder (optional for spice lovers)
- Salt and pepper to taste
- Vegetable oil for cooking

Instructions:

1. Heat some vegetable oil in a large pan and sauté the chopped onions until golden brown.

2. Add the minced garlic and sauté for another minute.

3. Mix in the tomato puree and bell pepper puree, stirring well.

4. Add the curry powder, thyme, paprika, and chili powder (if desired). Season with salt and pepper.

5. Add the rice and stir well, ensuring it is evenly coated with the sauce.

6. Pour enough water into the pan to cover the rice entirely, about 1 inch above the rice level.

7. Cover the pan and let the rice cook on low heat for about 20-25 minutes, or until the rice is tender and cooked through.

8. Serve the Jollof rice hot with grilled chicken, fish, or any preferred side dish.

2. Injera (Ethiopia/Eritrea):

Injera is a sourdough flatbread with a unique, spongy texture, and it holds significant symbolism in Ethiopian and Eritrean cultures. The large, round form of injera represents community and togetherness. Traditionally, a large piece of injera serves as a communal dining plate, topped with various stews, curries, or vegetables. Eating injera involves breaking off small pieces with the hands, fostering a sense of sharing and unity.

Ingredients:

- 3 cups of Teff flour (or substitute with a mix of whole wheat and all-purpose flour)

- 3 cups of water

- 1/2 teaspoon of yeast (optional)

- Salt to taste

- Cooking oil for greasing the pan

Instructions:

1. In a large bowl, mix the teff flour and water, slowly incorporating them together until you have a smooth batter.

2. If using yeast, add it to the mixture and let it sit covered for a few hours or overnight to allow fermentation (optional but enhances flavor).

3. Stir in some salt to taste.

4. Heat a non-stick skillet or injera pan over medium heat and lightly grease it with oil.

5. Pour about a quarter to a half cup of the batter onto the pan, then quickly tilt and rotate the pan to spread the batter into a thin, large circular shape.

6. Cover the pan to allow the injera to cook for a few minutes until the edges lift up, and the surface is firm but not crispy.

7. Remove the injera from the pan and let it cool on a clean cloth or serving plate.

8. Repeat the process until you have utilized all the batter, stacking each injera on top of the other.

9. Serve the injera with various stews, curries, or vegetables, placing them on top of the injera and tearing pieces off to enjoy communally.

These examples and recipes uncover just a fraction of the rich symbolism present in African cuisine. From the vibrant colors to the communal eating traditions, African dishes are a celebration of culture, history, and shared experiences.

Chapter 6: The Ingredients of African Cuisine- The selection and preparation of ingredients in African cuisine

African cuisine is known for its diverse flavors, use of spices, and vibrant colors. The continent's rich biodiversity provides Africans with a wide range of fresh ingredients to create their culinary masterpieces. In this chapter, we will delve deep into the selection and preparation of ingredients in African cuisine, exploring the unique aspects that make it so enticing.

1. Staple Foods:

African cuisine heavily relies on staple foods that form the foundation of most meals. These include maize (corn), millet, sorghum, yams, cassava, and plantains. These ingredients are not only readily available but also play a significant role in ensuring food security across the continent.

1.1 Maize (Corn):

Maize, also known as corn, is a primary staple food in many African countries. It is used to make various dishes such as porridge (pap), cornbread, and even alcoholic beverages. Maize is ground into flour to make pastes and dough for bread and other baked goods.

1.2 Millet and Sorghum:

Millet and sorghum are gluten-free grains that are widely consumed in Africa. They are used to make kulikuli (groundnut cakes), millet porridge, or pounded into a fine flour for making thick stews and porridges.

1.3 Yams, Cassava, and Plantains:

Yams, cassava, and plantains are starchy vegetables that are often boiled, fried, or pounded into a paste. These ingredients are versatile and can be used in various dishes, including yam pottage, cassava fufu, and fried plantains.

2. Protein Sources:

Protein-rich ingredients play a vital role in African cuisine, providing essential nutrients and adding depth of flavor to dishes. Here are some notable protein sources used:

2.1 Meat and Poultry:

Meat and poultry are commonly used in African cuisine. Beef, goat, lamb, and chicken are prepared in different ways, including grilling, stewing, or roasting. In West Africa, special emphasis is given to goat meat, which is regarded as a delicacy.

2.2 Fish and Seafood:

With abundant coastlines and inland bodies of water, fish and seafood are significant parts of African diets. Tilapia, catfish, mackerel, and shrimp are among the popular choices, often cooked in stews or grilled.

2.3 Legumes:

Beans, lentils, and peanuts (groundnuts) are essential sources of protein, especially for vegetarians and vegans. They are used in a variety of dishes, such as bean stews, peanut soups, and lentil salads.

3. Fresh Produce and Seasonings:

Fresh produce plays a crucial role in African cuisine in terms of both taste and nutrition. The continent's diverse climate allows for the cultivation of a wide array of fruits, vegetables, and herbs. Some noteworthy ingredients include:

3.1 Leafy Greens:

Many varieties of leafy greens, such as amaranth, spinach, and okra leaves, are used extensively in African cooking. They are often sautéed with spices or included in stews and soups.

3.2 Root Vegetables:

In addition to yams and cassava, African cuisine incorporates root vegetables like sweet potatoes, cocoyams, and taro. These vegetables are celebrated for their mildly sweet taste and high nutritional value.

3.3 Indigenous Fruits:

Africa boasts an abundance of exotic fruits, including mangoes, guavas, papayas, and baobab fruit. These fruits, both consumed fresh and used in various recipes, add refreshing flavors to African dishes.

3.4 Herbs and Spices:

Herbs and spices are the soul of African cuisine, enhancing the taste and aroma of dishes. Some commonly used spices include ginger, garlic, chili peppers, cinnamon, cardamom, and cloves. Traditional herb blends like berbere (Ethiopia) and suya spice (West Africa) are also widely employed.

THE SELECTION AND PREPARATION of ingredients in African cuisine define its unique flavors and culinary traditions. From staple foods like maize and millet to protein sources such as meat, fish, and legumes, African cuisine encompasses a variety of ingredients. The rich diversity of fresh produce and spices adds depth and complexity to each dish. Understanding the significance of these ingredients is key to appreciating the multifaceted nature of African cuisine.

- The uses and benefits of ingredients in African cuisine

African cuisine is known for its rich and diverse flavors. The continent's vast and varied landscapes have influenced the ingredients used in traditional African dishes. These ingredients not only contribute to the unique taste and aromas found in African cuisine but also offer various health benefits.

One popular ingredient found in many African dishes is the yam. Yams are a versatile root vegetable that can be boiled, roasted, or mashed. They are a great source of carbohydrates, making them a staple in many African diets. Yams are also packed with essential vitamins and minerals such as vitamin C, potassium, and manganese. These nutrients promote healthy bones, improve immune function, and contribute to overall health and well-being.

Another commonly used ingredient in African cooking is red palm oil. This oil is derived from the fruit of the oil palm tree. Red palm oil is rich in antioxidants, including beta-carotene and vitamin E. These antioxidants help fight inflammation and protect the body against oxidative damage. Red palm oil also contains healthy fats, including monounsaturated and polyunsaturated fats, which can help improve heart health when consumed as part of a balanced diet.

Leafy greens are integral to African cuisine, and one popular green is kale. Kale is a nutrient powerhouse, packed with vitamins A, C, and K. It is also a great source of fiber, calcium, and iron. These nutrients support healthy digestion, boost the immune system, and promote bone and cardiovascular health. Additionally, kale is known for its anti-inflammatory properties, making it an excellent addition to a healthy diet.

Another ingredient with immense dietary and medicinal benefits is the moringa tree. Moringa leaves are highly nutritious, containing significant amounts of vitamins, minerals, and antioxidants. They are known for their ability to fight inflammation, lower blood sugar levels, and improve digestive health. The moringa tree is often called the "tree of life," as nearly all parts of the plant- leaves, pods, roots, and seeds- have medicinal properties.

Spices play a crucial role in African cuisine, adding depth and complexity to dishes. One commonly used spice is chili powder, made from ground chili peppers. Chili powder contains capsaicin, which gives it its spicy kick. Capsaicin has been shown to boost metabolism, reduce appetite, and reduce inflammation. It may also have antimicrobial and cancer-fighting properties, making it a powerful ingredient with both culinary and health benefits.

Lastly, the use of peanuts in African cuisine provides a tasty and nutritious addition. Peanuts are an excellent source of plant-based protein, healthy fats, and essential vitamins and minerals. They are rich in antioxidants that help protect against heart disease and control blood sugar levels. Peanuts are also an excellent source of resveratrol, a compound that has been linked to improved heart health and reduced risk of certain cancers.

In conclusion, African cuisine incorporates a wide range of ingredients that not only enhance the flavors of dishes but also offer numerous health benefits. From yams and red palm oil to kale and moringa, the ingredients commonly used in African cooking provide essential nutrients, promote healthful benefits, and contribute to the diversity and richness of this incredible culinary tradition.

- The examples and recipes of dishes that showcase the ingredients of African cuisine

African cuisine is known for its vibrant and diverse flavors, which are brought to life with a blend of fresh ingredients, aromatic spices, and traditional cooking techniques. From the scorching deserts of North Africa to the lush rainforests of Central Africa, each region has its own unique culinary heritage.

One of the most beloved ingredients in African cuisine is the humble yam. Often referred to as the "king of roots," yams are a staple in many African households. They are versatile, nutritious, and play a crucial role in African cuisine. Yams can be boiled, mashed, roasted, or turned into a delicious filling for pies and fritters.

An example of a dish that beautifully showcases the use of yams is the popular Nigerian dish, Yam Porridge. This hearty one-pot meal combines diced yams, tomatoes, onions, peppers, and various spices. The yams are slowly simmered in a flavorful sauce until they become tender and soak up all the aromatic flavors. Yam Porridge is often enjoyed with a side of fresh vegetables or a protein such as fish or chicken.

Moving onto East Africa, the staple ingredient in the region is maize, or corn. In countries like Kenya or Tanzania, you will commonly find dishes such as Ugali, which is a staple side dish made from maize flour. Ugali is similar to polenta in texture and is typically served with grilled meats, stews, or sautéed vegetables. It acts as a perfect base to soak up the rich flavors of the accompanying dishes.

In West Africa, the use of plantains shines through in various recipes. Plantains are a member of the banana family but are much larger and starchier. They can be cooked in a multitude of ways, from frying to boiling and grilling. One classic dish that showcases the use of plantains is the West African delicacy called Kelewele. This street food favorite features ripe plantains cut into cubes and seasoned with a blend of spices like ginger, nutmeg, and chili flakes before being deep-fried to a crispy perfection.

Finally, in the southern parts of Africa, you can't escape the influence of delicious braais, or barbecues. One popular ingredient in southern African cuisine that shines during these gatherings is known as biltong. Biltong is a dried, cured meat that is similar to beef jerky. It is often made from venison or beef and is marinated in a blend of spices before being air-dried for several days. The result is a tender and flavorful meat that is enjoyed as a snack or as an accompaniment to beer at social gatherings.

These are just a few examples of the vast array of ingredients and dishes that showcase the richness of African cuisine. From yams to maize, plantains to biltong, African cuisine truly embraces the variety and abundance of the continent's resources. Whether you're a seasoned cook or a curious food enthusiast, exploring the flavors of African cuisine is sure to be a delightful and palate-pleasing adventure.

Chapter 7: The Techniques of African Cuisine- The tools and methods of cooking in African cuisine

African cuisine is rich in diverse flavors and techniques, offering a culinary experience like no other. In this chapter, we will explore the tools and methods used in African cooking, revealing the intricate artistry and innovation behind these traditional culinary practices. From ingenious cooking implements to sophisticated techniques, let us embark on a journey into the heart of African cuisine.

1. Traditional African Cooking Tools:

African cooking is deeply rooted in centuries-old traditions, and the tools used reflect this deep connection to history and culture. Here are some of the traditional cooking tools commonly utilized in African cuisine:

a. Mortar and Pestle:

The mortar and pestle form an essential part of African kitchens, used for pounding and mashing a variety of ingredients. Made from materials such as wood, clay, or stone, the mortar and pestle facilitate the grinding of spices, herbs, and grains, creating aromatic pastes and powders integral to African dishes.

b. Clay Pots:

Clay pots are indispensable cooking vessels in many African households. These pots are crafted by hand using locally sourced clay, providing a natural and effective means of slow cooking. Clay pots distribute heat evenly, enhancing the flavors of stews, soups, and braised meats, while retaining moisture to create tender and succulent dishes.

c. Grilling Baskets:

Grilling is an integral part of African cooking, and grilling baskets, made from bamboo or stainless steel wires, are commonly used to roast meats and vegetables over an open flame. These baskets offer the perfect platform to cook food evenly, imparting a delicious smoky flavor to the dish.

2. African Culinary Techniques:

African cuisine encompasses a wide range of culinary techniques, all contributing to the varied and vibrant flavors found in traditional dishes. Here are some noteworthy techniques:

a. Slow Cooking:

Slow cooking is central to African cuisine, as it allows flavors to meld together and intensify. By cooking ingredients over low heat for extended periods, whether in clay pots or cast-iron stoves, rich and complex flavors develop, resulting in stews and sauces that are deeply satisfying.

b. Peanut Sauce:

Peanut sauce is a classic technique widely appreciated in West African cooking. Roasted peanuts are ground to a fine paste using a mortar and pestle, then cooked slowly with an array of spices and herbs to create a luscious and savory sauce. This technique enhances the nutty undertones and adds a distinctive creaminess to the dishes.

c. Fermentation:

Fermentation is prevalent in African cuisine, playing a crucial role in adding depth and complexity to flavors. Popular ferments include fermented maize, millet, teff, and cassava, which are used in various dishes, such as injera (Ethiopian fermented flatbread) or ogi (Nigerian fermented cereal pudding). Fermentation not only imparts unique flavors but also enhances the nutritional value of the food.

AS WE CONCLUDE OUR exploration of African culinary techniques, we have unraveled the essential tools and methods prevalent in African cuisine. From the use of traditional cooking implements like mortars and clay pots to techniques like slow cooking and fermentation, African cuisine showcases a harmonious blend of tradition and innovation. By understanding and appreciating these techniques, one gains a deeper appreciation for the vibrant flavors and intricate artistry of African cooking.

- The skills and innovations of cooking in African cuisine

African cuisine is a rich and diverse tapestry of flavors, textures, and ingredients. The continent's culinary traditions reflect a complex amalgamation of cultures, histories, and natural resources, resulting in unique and delicious dishes. Central to the skill and innovation of African cooking are several key elements that elevate it to a level worthy of exploration.

One fundamental aspect of African cuisine lies in its extensive use of native ingredients. The continent's incredible biodiversity offers a multitude of raw materials that are transformed into delectable dishes. From leafy greens like amaranth and moringa, to starchy staples like cassava, yams, and plantains, African cooks have a wealth of ingredients at their disposal. These elements form the backbone of many traditional recipes and provide a distinct flavor profile that is deeply rooted in their respective regions.

Moreover, African cuisine boasts numerous cooking techniques that have been perfected over centuries. Take, for example, the art of grilling. Across the continent, open-fire grilling is a common way of preparing meat, fish, and vegetables. By carefully charring the ingredients over the flames, African cooks infuse rich smoky flavors into their dishes. This unique technique creates a depth of flavor that is often difficult to achieve through other means of preparation.

Innovation is also a prevalent characteristic of African cooking. Despite the strong ties to tradition, African chefs are constantly exploring and experimenting with new ways to enhance their dishes. This innovative approach can be seen in the incorporation of fusion cooking. Some chefs blend African flavors with those from other regions, resulting in delightful culinary fusions. For example, West African jollof rice has become popular internationally for its blend of spices and caramelized textures.

Furthermore, African cuisine is redefining what it means to eat sustainably. The use of local and seasonal ingredients minimizes the ecological impact and encourages a closer connection to regional food systems. Sustainable agricultural practices, such as organic farming, agroforestry, and permaculture, are gaining traction as people recognize the importance of preserving African soil and biodiversity.

The skills required to master African cuisine are usually passed down from one generation to the next. Traditional techniques are taught within families and communities, ensuring the preservation of cultural heritage. However, modern training schools and culinary institutions are now cropping up across the continent, offering platforms for aspiring chefs to refine their skills and innovate with African flavors.

In conclusion, the skill and innovation found in African cooking stem from its use of native ingredients, mastery of traditional techniques, culinary fusion, and its commitment to sustainable practices. This cuisine celebrates, preserves, and elevates the diverse flavors of Africa while embracing the future. Exploring African cuisine is a journey that leads to not only gastronomic delights but also a deeper appreciation for the complexities of the continent's culinary traditions.

- The examples and recipes of dishes that showcase the techniques of African cuisine

African cuisine is as diverse as the continent itself. With over 50 countries and thousands of ethnic groups, each region boasts its own traditional dishes and unique cooking techniques. From North Africa's fragrant spice blends to West Africa's rich peanut-based stews, there is an abundance of mouth-watering dishes to explore. In this article, we will delve into some examples and recipes that showcase the techniques of African cuisine.

1. Jollof Rice (West Africa):

Jollof Rice is a popular dish found in many West African countries like Nigeria, Senegal, and Ghana. This one-pot rice dish is made with parboiled rice cooked in a flavorful tomato-based sauce. The technique for this dish involves frying onions and garlic, then adding tomato paste and spices before cooking the rice in the sauce. It is often served with grilled chicken or fish and spicy plantains.

2. Tagine (North Africa):

Tagine is a traditional Moroccan dish cooked in a clay pot with a conical lid, also called a tagine. The slow-cooking technique allows the flavors of the aromatic spices and ingredients to meld together. Tagine can be made with various meat or vegetable combinations such as lamb with prunes, chicken with preserved lemons, or vegetables with chickpeas. The result is a tender and aromatic dish that is usually served with couscous.

3. Bunny Chow (South Africa):

Bunny Chow is a unique and popular street food in South Africa, particularly in Durban. Originally designed as a portable meal for Indian sugar cane workers, a Bunny Chow consists of a hollowed-out loaf of bread filled with a spicy curry. The curry can be vegetarian, chicken, or lamb, and it is often accompanied by pickles and grated carrot. This dish is a fusion of Indian flavors and African convenience.

4. Berbere-Spiced Chicken (East Africa):

Berbere is a traditional Ethiopian spice blend that is used to season many dishes. One delicious example is Berbere-Spiced Chicken, where chicken pieces are marinated in a paste made of berbere spice, garlic, lemon juice, and olive oil. The chicken is then grilled or roasted to perfection, resulting in a flavorful and tender dish. It is typically served with injera, a sourdough flatbread, and a variety of colorful vegetable and legume stews.

5. Bobotie (Southern Africa):

Bobotie is a classic dish from South Africa that combines sweet and savory flavors. It is a spiced minced meat dish topped with an egg-based custard and baked until golden brown. This dish originated from the Cape Malay community and is made with various spices like curry powder, turmeric, and cumin. Bobotie is typically served with yellow rice, chutney, and a variety of sidedishes.

These examples and recipes highlight the diverse and rich techniques of African cuisine. From slow-cooking in a clay pot to marinating meat in aromatic spice blends, African cooking celebrates the vibrant flavors and culinary traditions of the continent. Whether you're a seasoned home cook or a culinary enthusiast, exploring the techniques of African cuisine will undoubtedly add a new dimension to your culinary repertoire.

Chapter 8: The Flavors of African Cuisine- The spices and herbs that enhance African cuisine

African cuisine is renowned for its rich and diverse flavors, which are achieved through the expert use of various spices and herbs. These aromatic ingredients play a crucial role in enhancing the taste, adding depth, and creating a sensory delight in African dishes. In this chapter, we will take an in-depth look at the spices and herbs commonly used in African cooking, exploring their unique properties and how they contribute to the flavors that define African cuisine.

1. Berbere:

Starting with a staple spice blend in Ethiopian and Eritrean cuisines, berbere encompasses a symphony of flavors with its bold mixture of spices. It typically includes a combination of red chili peppers, garlic, ginger, fenugreek, cardamom, coriander, cinnamon, and cloves. Berbere adds a complex heat and earthiness to stews, meats, and various lentil dishes commonly found in these regions, making it an indispensable element in their traditional cuisine.

2. Ras el Hanout:

Originating from North Africa, Ras el Hanout is a spice blend that literally translates to "top of the shop" or referring to the best spices a merchant has to offer. Its ingredients may vary, but it often includes cardamom, cumin, clove, cinnamon, nutmeg, ginger, turmeric, and paprika. Ras el Hanout adds an aromatic complexity and depth of flavor to dishes like tagines, couscous, and roasted meats, giving them a distinctly North African taste.

3. Njangsa:

Njangsa is a West African spice also known as "sese" or "akpi." It comes from the seeds of the Ricinodendron heudelotii tree and possesses a nutty and slightly sweet flavor. Commonly used in traditional soups, stews, and sauces, Njangsa adds a robust taste while enhancing the overall aroma of the dishes.

4. Bitterleaf:

As the name suggests, bitterleaf is an herb that adds a distinct bitter flavor to African dishes. It is derived from the Vernonia amygdalina plant and is particularly popular in West African cuisine. Bitterleaf is often used in soups, stews, and traditional herbal drinks. Its sharp taste provides a balance to the richness of the other ingredients in the dish, making it an essential component in the flavor profile of many African recipes.

5. Suya Spice:

Suya spice is a popular Nigerian spice blend that is primarily used to marinate and flavor skewered meats, such as beef, chicken, or goat. This blend typically consists of ground peanuts, garlic, ginger, paprika, cayenne pepper, and onion powder. When used in cooking, it imparts a vibrant and tangy flavor to the meat, highlighting the smoky and spicy notes that African cuisine is known for.

6. Calabash Nutmeg:

Calabash nutmeg, also called ehuru or nkolika in different African regions, is derived from the seeds of the Monodora myristica tree. This spice has a pungent aroma reminiscent of nutmeg, but with a richer and more intense flavor. It is widely used in West African soups, stews, and sauces, adding a robust taste and earthy undertones.

SPICES AND HERBS HOLD a special place in African cuisine, transforming ordinary dishes into extraordinary culinary delights. From the warmth of berbere to the complexity of Ras el Hanout, the unique combination of flavors derived from the spices and herbs ingrained in African cooking reflects the diversity and richness of the African continent. Exploring and experimenting with these ingredients allows us to truly appreciate the authenticity and cultural significance behind African cuisine.

- The sauces and condiments that complement African cuisine

African cuisine is renowned for its vibrant flavors, fragrant spices, and unique combinations, and one of the secrets behind its deliciousness lies in the array of sauces and condiments that bring its dishes to life. These accompaniments play a crucial role in enhancing the taste, texture, and overall experience of African culinary delights, creating a harmonious fusion of savory, sweet, spicy, and tangy elements.

One of the most commonly used condiments in African cuisine is peri-peri sauce, also known as piri-piri. This fiery chili sauce originated in Mozambique but is now popular across the continent. Made from hot red chilies, garlic, lemon juice, and sometimes oils like olive or vegetable, peri-peri sauce adds a kick to grilled meats, fish, or even vegetables. It pairs particularly well with South African grilled peri-peri chicken, giving it a complex and zesty flavor. The heat from the peri-peri sauce is both tantalizingly spicy and incredibly addictive; Africans claim that the peri-peri bite never fails to leave a lasting impression.

Moving away from intense spiciness to a more aromatic note, harissa is another staple sauce in North African cuisine. A signature of Tunisia, this paste-like condiment combines roasted red peppers, hot chili peppers, garlic, and spices such as cumin and coriander. The result is a rich and smoky flavor profile that adds depth to dishes like couscous, tagines, and grilled meats. From Tunisian street food stalls to high-end restaurants, harissa is a versatile companion that infuses warmth and complexity into every dish it graces.

For those seeking bold and robust flavors, suya spice is African cuisine's answer. Originating from Nigeria, suya is a dry rub made from ground peanuts, ginger, garlic, chili powder, and a blend of traditional Yoruba spices. The spiced peanut mix is then sprinkled over skewered protein, be it beef, chicken, or goat, and grilled to perfection. Suya spice not only adds an irresistible crunch to the dish but also evokes a sense of warmth and homeliness. The peanuts create a distinctive earthiness, while the spices provide a balancing heat that is sure to delight the taste buds.

Shito, a Ghanaian black pepper sauce with a very distinct flavor, is a must-mention when talking about African condiments. This versatile sauce is made by infusing ingredients like fish, shrimp, or meat with black pepper, dried chili flakes, ginger, garlic, and a blend of spices. This mixture is then cooked down until it transforms into a thick and savory sauce that's incredibly fragrant and tangy. Skewered kebabs, jollof rice, or even fried plantains find their perfect complement in the umami-packed richness of shito. Its unique flavor often leaves newcomers pleasantly surprised and eager to explore more of African cuisine.

Lastly, no discussion about African condiments would be complete without mentioning the renowned peri-peri chutney of South Africa. This tangy and sweet condiment has a distinct flavor profile owing to its key ingredients: vinegar, sugar, and a hint of garlic. The recipe often presents regional variations, with subtle tweaks made to give the chutney a unique touch. From hot and spicy to tangy and subtly sweet, peri-peri chutney's versatility knows no bounds. It imparts acidity and brightness to an assortment of dishes, including stews, braises, and grilled meats, and its flavorful punch elevates even the simplest of ingredients to new gastronomic heights.

In conclusion, African cuisine is elevated to new heights with the addition of these remarkable sauces and condiments. From the fiery kick of peri-peri sauce to the fragrant complexity of harissa, the delectable. suya spice to the rich and tangy shito, and the timeless peri-peri chutney, these accompaniments compliment, balance, and enhance the diverse flavors present in African dishes. Whether they're providing a fiery touch, an enticing aroma, or a marriage of bold and tangy elements, these sauces and condiments ensure that African cuisine remains a tapestry of astonishing tastes and unforgettable culinary experiences.

- The examples and recipes of dishes that showcase the flavors of African cuisine

African cuisine is as diverse as the continent itself, with each region showcasing its own unique flavors and culinary traditions. From fragrant spice blends to hearty stews, here are some examples and recipes of dishes that highlight the rich flavors of African cuisine.

1. Jollof Rice (West Africa):

Jollof rice is a popular dish in many West African countries, known for its bright red color and delicious taste. It is commonly made with rice, tomatoes, onions, garlic, and a blend of spices such as thyme, curry powder, and bay leaves. Some variations may include protein sources like chicken, beef, or fish. This flavorful one-pot dish is a staple at social gatherings and celebrations in countries like Nigeria, Ghana, and Senegal.

2. Bobotie (South Africa):

Originating in Cape Malay cuisine, bobotie is a savory baked dish with a sweet and tangy flavor. It typically consists of spiced minced meat, usually lamb or beef, mixed with onions, garlic, dried fruit, and a blend of spices such as curry powder, turmeric, and coriander. The meat mixture is topped with a creamy egg custard and baked until golden brown. Bobotie is commonly served with yellow rice and chutney, creating a delicious combination of flavors.

3. Doro Wat (Ethiopia):

Doro Wat is a traditional Ethiopian dish that showcases the rich flavors of African spices. It is a spicy chicken stew made with chicken drumsticks or thighs, berbere spice blend (which includes chili peppers, garlic, ginger, and various herbs), onions, tomatoes, and clarified butter called niter kibbeh. Doro Wat is often served with injera, a sourdough flatbread, which complements the spicy stew and helps soothe the heat.

4. Moqueca de Camarão (Brazil):

Moqueca de Camarão is a delightful dish that combines African and Brazilian flavors. Originating in the northeastern state of Bahia, this shrimp stew is prepared using ingredients like coconut milk, palm oil, bell peppers, onions, garlic, and various spices. The flavors of lime juice, coriander, and dendê (palm oil) lend a unique taste and aroma to the dish. Moqueca de Camarão is often served with white rice and farofa (toasted cassava flour), making it a filling and flavorful meal.

5. Piri Piri Chicken (Mozambique):

Piri Piri chicken, also known as Peri-Peri chicken, is a popular grilled or roasted dish originating from Mozambique. It involves marinating chicken pieces in a spicy sauce made from African bird's eye chili peppers, garlic, lemon juice, paprika, and various herbs. The marinated chicken is then cooked to perfection, resulting in juicy and flavorful meat with a fiery kick. Piri Piri chicken is often accompanied by grilled vegetables or fries, allowing the flavors to shine through.

These are just a few examples of the diverse and flavorful dishes that exemplify African cuisine. Exploring the rich spices, traditional cooking techniques, and unique ingredients of African cuisine is a culinary journey that promises to delight food enthusiasts and expand their palates.

Chapter 9: The Staples of African Cuisine- The grains and cereals that sustain African cuisine

Africa is a continent renowned for its diverse and rich culinary heritage. At the heart of African cuisine are the staples that form the foundation of many traditional dishes. Grains and cereals, in particular, play a crucial role in African cooking, serving as the primary source of sustenance for millions of people across the continent. This chapter delves into the intricacies of the grains and cereals that sustain African cuisine, highlighting their importance, versatility, and cultural significance.

Maize (Corn):

Maize, also known as corn, holds exceptional prominence in African cooking. Introduced to Africa from the Americas during the colonial era, maize quickly adapted to the continent's diverse climates and find its home in various African countries. Maize is loved for its versatility, affordability, and nutritional value. It serves as a staple in many dishes, including the iconic Ugali in East Africa, Sadza in Southern Africa, and Nshima in Central Africa. These porridge-like preparations, made from cornmeal, accompany a wide array of stews, making for a hearty and filling meal.

Sorghum:

Sorghum is among the oldest known grains in Africa and has been a significant part of many indigenous cultures for centuries. This drought-resistant crop thrives in arid regions, where other grains struggle to survive. Sorghum is highly versatile, can be ground into flour or cooked whole, and is commonly used to make porridges, flatbreads, and beer. In West Africa, consumption of Sorghum is prevalent, particularly in countries like Niger and Mali, where dishes like Couscous de fonio (a millet-based dish) are traditional favorites.

Millet:

As one of the oldest grains cultivated by humanity, millet has shaped the culinary traditions of Africa for thousands of years. This hardy grain is highly adaptable and can be grown in a wide range of climates. The variations of millet used in African cuisine include pearl millet, finger millet, and foxtail millet. In regions such as Ethiopia, millet serves as the primary ingredient in Injera, the iconic fermented flatbread synonymous with Ethiopian cuisine. The grains are also used to prepare porridges and couscous-like dishes common in Central and West Africa.

Rice:

Rice, though not native to Africa, has been widely cultivated and enjoyed across the continent for centuries. Introduced through trade routes and colonial influence, rice has taken root particularly in West Africa, becoming a vital element of regional cuisine. Jollof rice, a flavorful one-pot rice dish cooked with various vegetables, spices, and meats, is a treasured specialty found in countries such as Nigeria, Senegal, and Ghana. Rice is also commonly used for vegetable and meat-based stews, creating a complete and satisfying meal.

THE GRAINS AND CEREALS that sustain African cuisine are not merely ingredients but carriers of centuries-old culinary traditions and cultural identity. From maize to sorghum, millet to rice, the utilization of these staples varies across the continent, with unique recipes and preparation methods defining each region's cuisine. Acknowledging the history and significance of these grains and cereals gives us a deeper appreciation for the rich tapestry of African culinary heritage. As the world increasingly seeks diverse and nutritious foods, African cuisine remains a reservoir of traditional knowledge that deserves exploration.

- The tubers and roots that nourish African cuisine

African cuisine is renowned for its rich and diverse flavors. One of the fundamental elements that contribute to the uniqueness and depth of African dishes are the tubers and roots used in traditional recipes. Although often overlooked, these plant-based ingredients play a significant role not only in nourishing African diets but also in capturing the essence of the continent's culinary traditions.

One of the key tubers that is widely consumed in various African countries is cassava. This starchy root plant is an essential source of carbohydrates for millions of people across the continent. It is extremely versatile and can be prepared in numerous ways. Cassava can be boiled, fried, or even fermented to make staple foods such as fufu, garri, and tapioca. Rich in fiber and essential nutrients like vitamin C, magnesium, and potassium, cassava is not only a filling food but also contributes to a balanced and wholesome African diet.

Yams are another significant tuber widely consumed in Africa. These tubers are a staple in West African cuisine. Yams not only possess a pleasant taste but also provide a good source of Vitamin C, potassium, and dietary fiber. They can be cooked through boiling, frying, or baking, and form the base of many dishes, including yam fries, pounded yam, and yam porridge. African cultures have also incorporated yams into traditional ceremonies and festivals, highlighting their cultural importance and symbolic value.

African cuisine also relies heavily on various root vegetables, such as sweet potatoes and taro. Sweet potatoes, with their vibrant orange flesh and sweet flavor, are a favorite ingredient in many African recipes. Whether roasted, boiled, or mashed, sweet potatoes add a distinct taste and nutritional value to African dishes. Packed with antioxidants, dietary fiber, and vitamins A and C, sweet potatoes are not only nourishing but also contribute to the vibrant and healthy appeal of African food.

Taro, often referred to as cocoyam in Africa, is another root vegetable that has made its mark in African kitchens. With its smooth texture and earthy flavor, taro is used in soups, stews, and even as a main ingredient in traditional dishes like Ekpang Nkukwo, a delicious Nigerian delicacy. Taro roots are rich in vitamins B and E, potassium, and dietary fiber, making them an excellent addition to a balanced diet.

Another noteworthy tuber frequently used in African cuisine is the African yam bean. This indigenous African plant produces tubers that are rich in protein and essential amino acids. These tubers are popular in various Nigerian dishes, such as porridges, fufu, and poricoke. African yam beans are not only a nutritional powerhouse but also an eco-friendly crop that helps maintain soil fertility and reduce reliance on chemical fertilizers.

In conclusion, the tubers and roots used in African cuisine serve as a testament to the continent's culinary diversity and nutrition. From the versatile cassava to the symbolic yam, the flavors of African dishes owe much to these humble yet nourishing ingredients. Whether boiled, fried, mashed, or stewed, these tubers and roots are a vital part of African culture and cuisine, providing both sustenance and delicious flavors that capture the essence of the continent's culinary traditions.

- The examples and recipes of dishes that showcase the staples of African cuisine

Exquisite Examples and Recipes of African Cuisine Staples

AFRICA, WITH ITS WIDESPREAD diversity of cultures and regions, boasts an astounding array of mouthwatering delicacies that hold a special place in the hearts and taste buds of its people. From the aromatic spices of North African cuisine to the hearty staples found in West Africa, the varied dishes present a remarkable tapestry of flavors and ingredients. In this article, we will delve into some exemplary examples and share delightful recipes showcasing the staples of African cuisine.

1. Jollof Rice – West Africa:

No exploration of African cuisine would be complete without mentioning Jollof Rice, a staple dish cherished in many West African households. Combining the richness of parboiled rice with a tantalizing blend of tomatoes, onions, peppers, and spices, Jollof Rice is a feast for the senses. This vibrant and flavorful one-pot wonder can be enjoyed on its own or served alongside fried plantains, grilled chicken, or fish.

Recipe:

- 2 cups parboiled rice
- 1 onion, finely chopped
- 2 tomatoes, chopped
- 1 bell pepper, diced
- 2 cloves garlic, minced
- 1 tablespoon tomato paste
- 1 teaspoon smoked paprika
- 1 teaspoon thyme
- 1 teaspoon curry powder
- 1 cup chicken or vegetable stock
- Salt and pepper to taste

- Vegetable oil

Instructions:

1. Heat oil in a large pan and sauté onion and garlic until translucent.

2. Add the tomatoes, bell pepper, tomato paste, and spices. Cook until the tomatoes break down and release their juices.

3. Stir in the rice and coat it thoroughly with the tomato mixture. Add the stock and bring it to a gentle boil.

4. Reduce the heat, cover the pan, and simmer the rice for about 20-25 minutes or until cooked and tender.

5. Fluff the rice with a fork and serve hot with your preferred accompaniments.

2. Tagine – North Africa:

Tagine, a traditional North African dish, is not just a cooking vessel but also the name for the aromatic slow-cooked dish it prepares. The Tajine primarily consists of tender meat or vegetables, layered with fragrant spices, dried fruits, and nuts, resulting in a flavor-packed and succulent stew. Popular varieties include lamb tagine with prunes, fish tagine with preserved lemons, and vegetable tagine with chickpeas.

Recipe (Vegetable Tagine):

- 1 eggplant, cubed
- 2 zucchinis, sliced
- 2 carrots, sliced
- 1 onion, finely chopped
- 3 garlic cloves, minced
- 1 can chickpeas, drained
- 2 teaspoons ground cumin
- 2 teaspoons ground coriander
- 1 teaspoon ground cinnamon
- 1 teaspoon paprika
- 1 cup vegetable broth
- Olive oil
- Salt and pepper to taste

Instructions:

1. Heat oil in a large tagine or skillet over medium heat. Sauté the onion and garlic until aromatic.

2. Add the eggplant, zucchini, and carrot. Cook until the vegetables are slightly tender.

3. Sprinkle with cumin, coriander, cinnamon, and paprika. Stir to evenly coat the vegetables with the spices.

4. Pour in the vegetable broth and drained chickpeas. Reduce heat, cover, and let it simmer for about 30-40 minutes or until the vegetables are cooked.

5. Season with salt and pepper, garnish with fresh herbs if desired, and serve hot alongside couscous or crusty bread.

AFRICAN CUISINE'S RICH tapestry thrives on the staples and ingredients that grace its diverse regions. Discovering the unique flavors and recipe traditions gives a glimpse into the deep-rooted culinary heritage nurtured throughout the continent. Whether savoring the aromatic Jollof Rice of West Africa or indulging in the fragrant Tagines of the North, African cuisine never fails to captivate the palates of food enthusiasts worldwide. So, spice up your next culinary adventure by incorporating the staples of African cuisine into your kitchen and experience the gastronomic delights for yourself.

Chapter 10: The Proteins of African Cuisine-The meat and poultry that enrich African cuisine

African cuisine is known for its flavor, diversity, and use of fresh ingredients. When it comes to proteins, African dishes are no exception. From succulent meat cooked over an open fire to tender poultry infused with aromatic spices, African cuisine offers a wide array of options to satisfy any meat lover's palate. In this chapter, we will explore the prominent role of meat and poultry in African cooking and discover the unique flavors they bring to the table.

The Traditional Meat Dishes:

Long before the advent of modern cooking techniques, Africans have been utilizing meat as an essential part of their diet. One renowned dish found in numerous African countries is Nyama Choma—a popular barbecue-style meat dish. It usually consists of marinated meat chunks, commonly beef, goat, or lamb, cooked slowly over an open fire. The result is a tender and flavorsome meat that forms the centerpiece of many African meals.

Several cultures in Africa also have traditional dishes featuring camel meat. Camel, being a source of sustenance and transportation in many arid regions, has found its place on the African culinary map. Dishes like Fréro in Chad or M'battan in Mali showcase the versatility of camel meat, which is often cooked with fragrant spices and herbs to create mouthwatering delicacies.

Exotic Game Meat:

African cuisine is renowned for incorporating exotic game meats into everyday meals. Hunters still contribute to the availability of game meat, which not only offers a unique taste but also adds an element of cultural heritage and adventure to the dining experience. From antelope to crocodile, zebra to hippopotamus, these meats provide rich flavors when combined with traditional African spices and cooking methods.

An emblematic example of African game meat is Wildebeest, which can be cooked in various ways, including grilling, stewing, or smoking. Its distinct flavor lies in its lean meat and wild origins. By combining ingredients like tomatoes, onions, and local spices, African cooks create remarkable dishes that are both tasty and nutritious.

Poultry Delicacies:

In addition to various meat options, poultry plays a crucial role in African cuisine. Chicken, in particular, is an integral part of many African dishes, accounting for its affordability and abundance. Popular dishes like Chicken Yassa from Senegal and Ethiopian Doro Wat showcase the range of flavors and cooking techniques that highlight African poultry offerings.

One remarkable aspect of African poultry preparation is the use of marinades and spice rubs, which elevate the flavors and tenderize the meat. For instance, Suya, a beloved Nigerian street food, features juicy skewered chicken bathed in a spice blend called yaji, consisting of ground peanuts, ginger, garlic, and chili powder, resulting in an explosion of flavors.

Sustainability and Ethical Considerations:

As African cuisine gains international popularity, it is crucial to approach the consumption of meat and poultry with an understanding of sustainability and ethical considerations. While game meats and traditional practices still hold cultural significance, measures should be taken to preserve wildlife populations and protect endangered species. Additionally, the use of antibiotic-free poultry and supporting local, ethically sourced meat can help address environmental concerns and promote sustainable practices.

MEAT AND POULTRY FORM the backbone of African cuisine, enriching it with diverse flavors and textures. From tender grilled meat to exotic game and mouthwatering poultry dishes, African proteins offer a world of culinary adventure. As we explore the intricate balance between tradition and sustainability, the richness of African cuisine continues to captivate and delight food enthusiasts worldwide.

- The fish and seafood that diversify African cuisine

Fish and seafood play a significant role in the diversified cuisine of Africa. With its vast coastline and abundance of freshwater bodies, the continent is home to a wide variety of species that are a staple in many African diets. From the vibrant markets in Senegal to the bustling fishing villages in Mozambique, fish and seafood hold a special place in the hearts and stomachs of Africans.

One of the most popular African fish dishes is grilled whole fish. Throughout the continent, you can find local fishermen grilling freshly caught fish on open fires by the seaside or in the bustling streets of coastal towns. This dish showcases the simplicity of African cooking, where the natural flavors of the fish are allowed to shine through. The choice of fish varies depending on the region, with tilapia, red snapper, and Nile perch being commonly used in West, East, and Central Africa, respectively.

Another iconic African fish dish is fish stew. This hearty and aromatic dish is created by simmering fish along with an array of spices, vegetables, and palm oil. Each country puts its own spin on the dish, resulting in a myriad of flavors and textures. In Nigeria, for example, Egusi soup is a popular fish stew made with the ground seeds of melon or squash, while in Senegal, Thieboudienne is a national dish often prepared with fish, rice, and vegetables, flavored with tamarind and various local spices.

In addition to freshwater fish, seafood is also prevalent in many African cuisines, particularly along the coastlines. The abundant waters of the Atlantic Ocean, the Indian Ocean, and the Mediterranean offer a wide variety of seafood options. From lobster to shrimp to squid, there is no shortage of delectable options for seafood lovers.

One classic African seafood dish that deserves a mention is the delectable Mozambican peri-peri prawns. These succulent prawns are marinated in a fiery peri-peri sauce, made from local chili peppers, garlic, lemon, and various herbs and spices. Grilled to perfection, they offer a mouthwatering combination of smoky flavors and spicy heat.

Moving inland, freshwater delicacies such as Nile perch, catfish, and crayfish take center stage. These species are abundant in the many lakes, rivers, and waterways that span across the continent. In countries like Uganda and Tanzania, fish from Lake Victoria is a popular choice, often fried and served with a side of ugali, a staple cornmeal dish.

It's worth noting that fish and seafood in Africa are more than just a source of sustenance; they are also deeply entrenched in cultural traditions and customs. In many coastal communities, fishing is not only a means of livelihood but also a way of life, with generations passing down fishing techniques and culinary expertise. Fish festivals and seafood markets attract locals and tourists alike, offering not just a delicious meal but also a glimpse into the vibrant culinary heritage of the continent.

In conclusion, the fish and seafood that diversify African cuisine are a testament to the natural bounties that surround the continent. From grilled whole fish to fish stew to peri-peri prawns, each dish reflects the rich cultural tapestry of Africa. Whether enjoyed by the seashore or in the heartland, fish and seafood play a significant role in nourishing both the body and the soul of Africans.

- The examples and recipes of dishes that showcase the proteins of African cuisine

African cuisine is known for its rich and diverse range of proteins. From traditional dishes made with meats like beef, lamb, and goat, to creative recipes using unique seafood and plant-based sources, African cuisines never fail to impress with their protein-packed offerings. Here, we explore some examples and recipes of dishes that perfectly showcase the proteins found in African cuisine.

1. Jollof Rice with Chicken:

Jollof Rice is a beloved West African dish known for its aromatic flavors and vibrant orange hue. The dish showcases both the utility and deliciousness of chicken as a protein source. To make Jollof Rice, start by browning chicken pieces in a hot pan with oil. Remove chicken and set aside. In the same pan, sauté onions, garlic, ginger, and chili until fragrant. Add tomato puree, paprika, cayenne pepper, thyme, bay leaves, and chicken stock. Stir in rice and simmer with the lid on until the rice is cooked and seasoned. Finally, serve the Jollof Rice with the juicy browned chicken pieces on top.

2. Doro Wat (Ethiopian Chicken Stew):

Doro Wat is a hearty and spicy chicken stew originating from Ethiopia. This protein-packed dish features tender and flavorful chicken in a rich stew made with red chili paste, onions, garlic, and various spices. Traditionally, it is served with injera, a type of flatbread. To make Doro Wat, start by marinating chicken drumsticks and thighs in a blend of lemon juice, berbere spice mix, salt, and pepper. Sear the chicken in a large pot with oil until browned, then remove and sauté onions until golden. Add garlic, ginger, and the berbere spice mix, and cook until fragrant. Stir in tomato paste, chicken stock, and return the chicken to the pot. Simmer for 30-40 minutes until the chicken is tender and the sauce has thickened.

3. Bobotie (South African Meatloaf):

Bobotie is a classic dish in South African cuisine that combines ground meat, spices, eggs, and a fragrant curry-like flavor. Usually made with beef, lamb, or a mixture of both, this protein-rich meatloaf is perfect for a comforting meal. To make Bobotie, start by sautéing onions and garlic until soft. Add ground meat (beef or lamb) alongside curry powder, turmeric, coriander, chutney, and Worcestershire sauce. Cook until the meat is browned, then transfer it to a baking dish. Combine milk, eggs, salt, and pepper in a separate bowl, then pour the mixture over the meat. Bake in the oven until the egg topping has set and turned golden. Serve the Bobotie with yellow rice, chutney, and sliced almonds for a complete meal.

4. Grilled Nigerian Suya Skewers:

Suya, a Nigerian street food delicacy, consists of skewered meat marinated in a spicy peanut blend and then grilled to perfection. Traditionally made with beef, this scrumptious protein-filled dish encompasses the flavors of West Africa. To make Suya, start by soaking wooden skewers in water to prevent burning. Combine roasted peanuts, ground ginger, garlic powder, paprika, cayenne pepper, and bouillon powder in a blender, and blend until powdered. Thread beef strips onto the skewers, then brush with oil and sprinkle the peanut spice blend generously. Grill the skewers on a high flame for a few minutes per side until cooked through, and serve with sliced onions, tomatoes, and a sprinkle of additional spice mix for extra heat.

5. Moroccan Seafood Tagine:

Moroccan cuisine embraces the wealth of seafood available along the country's coastline. This seafood tagine highlights the nutritional benefits of proteins such as fish, shrimp, and shellfish, while infusing Moroccan flavors. Begin by sautéing onions, garlic, and spices like turmeric, paprika, and ginger in an oiled tagine or a large pot with a lid. Add diced tomatoes, tomato paste, and a fish or seafood stock, and let it simmer for a few minutes. Place your choice of fish fillets, shrimp, mussels, or clams on top of the tomato and onion mixture. Cover with the tagine lid and gently simmer for around 10-15 minutes until the seafood is cooked through. Serve the seafood tagine hot alongside couscous or crusty bread.

These examples and recipes only scratch the surface of the immense variety of proteins utilized in African cuisine. Exploring the culinary landscapes of Africa will not only introduce you to new and exciting flavors but also open your eyes to the various sources of protein that are abundantly incorporated into the dishes. Whether it's meats, seafood, or plant-based proteins, African cuisine takes pride in its delectable and diverse range of protein-packed meals.

Chapter 11: The Vegetables of African Cuisine- The greens and legumes that balance African cuisine

African cuisine is a treasure trove of vibrant flavors and diverse ingredients. While many people commonly associate African food with meat-based dishes, the continent also boasts an impressive array of vegetables. In this chapter, we will explore the greens and legumes that bring balance, color, and nutritional benefits to African cuisine.

1. African Leafy Greens:

A staple in African diets, leafy greens play a crucial role in providing essential nutrients such as iron, calcium, vitamins A, C, and K. These greens are often cooked and consumed as a side dish, soup, or mixed with other ingredients to create a flavorful delight. Here are some of the well-known African leafy greens:

a. Amaranth:

Also known as "hirse" or "terere," amaranth is a leafy green that comes in various forms, including red, green, and black. It is versatile and can be used in salads, sautés, or soups.

b. African Spinach:

Native to West and Central Africa, African spinach, or "pondu," is a nutritious leafy green that adds a mild, earthy taste to dishes. It can be cooked with tomatoes, onions, and seasonings to create a delightful accompaniment to meat or fish.

c. Waterleaf:

Waterleaf, or "gbure" in Nigeria, is a popular vegetable found across the continent. It has a high water content and a unique taste that enhances stews, soups, and traditional African sauces.

2. Nutritious Legumes:

Legumes play a critical role in African cuisine by providing protein, fiber, and essential minerals. They are often used to make stews, soups, spreads, and even pastes. Let's explore some notable legumes used in African cooking:

a. Cowpeas:

Also known as black-eyed peas, cowpeas are a versatile legume that features in dishes throughout the African continent. They are the main ingredient in one-pot wonder dishes like akara (bean cakes) and moin moin (steamed bean pudding).

b. Bambara Groundnut:

Indigenous to Africa, the bambara groundnut is a nutritious legume that is rich in protein, fiber, and various essential minerals. It is often roasted, boiled, or ground into flour to make traditional dishes like kuli kuli (peanut snack) or snacks.

c. Lentils:

Although lentils are not originally from Africa, they have been widely adopted and incorporated into various African recipes. They are an excellent source of plant-based protein and are used in dishes like lentil stew, lentil fritters, and lentil soups.

3. The Balance in African Cuisine:

The inclusion of greens and legumes in African cuisine is not only about flavor but also about balance. With many meat-based dishes being rich and heavy, vegetables are essential for creating a well-rounded meal. The combination of meat, leafy greens, and legumes provides a diverse array of nutrients, ensuring a healthy and balanced diet.

IN THIS CHAPTER, WE have delved into the diverse world of African vegetables, exploring the leafy greens and legumes that bring harmony to African cuisine. From amaranth and African spinach to cowpeas and lentils, these ingredients contribute color, nutrition, and complex flavors to dishes across the continent. Understanding and appreciating the role of vegetables in African cuisine allows us to truly immerse ourselves in the culinary wonders of this rich and diverse culture.

- The fruits and nuts that sweeten African cuisine

When it comes to African cuisine, there is an incredible array of fruits and nuts that play a vital role in making dishes delectably sweet. These natural wonders not only add a burst of flavor to meals but also provide important nutritional benefits. From succulent tropical fruits to rich, buttery nuts, let's dive into the world of African sweeteners.

One of the fruits that steal the spotlight in African cuisine is the delectable baobab fruit. This superfood grows abundantly in various regions of Africa and is renowned for its tangy flavor. Known as the "tree of life," the baobab is packed with vitamin C, fiber, and antioxidants. African communities traditionally use its dried fruit pulp to sweeten dishes ranging from soups to desserts. Its unique taste brings a delightful tartness to the table, giving culinary creations a burst of freshness.

Moving south, we encounter the small yet exceptionally succulent Marula fruit. Native to Southern and Western Africa, this fruit boasts a unique combination of fruity and nutty flavors. Rich in vitamin C, calcium, and proteins, Marula is not only sweet but also highly nutritious. With its sweet, delicate taste, it features in desserts like puddings and tarts. Moreover, its juicy pulp is a crucial ingredient in the much-loved Marula liqueur, a popular indulgence across the continent.

Another fruit synonymous with African sweetness is the baill fruit, predominantly found in West Africa. This yellow, tangy fruit is commonly used to flavor soups and sauces, especially in countries like Senegal and Guinea. Its distinct citrusy flavor balances the intensity of other ingredients and adds a refreshing twist to savory dishes.

African cuisine also celebrates the wonder of nuts. Take the velvety shea nut, for instance. The West African shea tree produces nuts that are crushed, roasted, and ground into a creamy paste. Recognized for its numerous health benefits, shea butter is often incorporated into desserts, giving them a nutty undertone and unmatched smoothness. The shea paste adds an element of indulgence to traditional African fritters, cookies, and candies, turning them into irresistible treats.

Next, we must mention the magnificent African oil palm and its invaluable contribution to sweetening African cuisine. This iconic fruit, native to tropical regions of West and Central Africa, provides not only oil but also a rich natural sweetener. The palm fruit's pulp is processed into a thick syrup or jaggery, which is widely used across Africa to sweeten porridges, pancakes, and baked goods. The distinct caramel-like flavor of palm syrup elevates dishes, making them a delight to the taste buds.

Beyond these flavorsome fruits and nuts, Africa also showcases countless other culinary treasures like tamarind, ginger, jujube, and more. These natural sweeteners add depth, richness, and complexity to African dishes, making them unique and irresistible.

As we explore the diverse range of fruits and nuts that sweeten African cuisine, we gain a deeper appreciation for the continent's impressive bounty. African culinary traditions shine a spotlight on these natural wonders, transforming simple meals into astonishing feasts for the senses. So, the next time you have the chance to savor African cuisine, remember to relish the sweetness infused by these delightful fruits and nuts.

- The examples and recipes of dishes that showcase the vegetables of African cuisine

African cuisine is a vibrant blend of flavors and ingredients, often incorporating an array of colorful vegetables. From the okra and sweet potatoes of West Africa to the leafy greens of East Africa, there is a wide variety of vegetables used in traditional African dishes. In this article, we will explore some examples and recipes of dishes that showcase the flavors and versatility of African vegetables.

1. Jollof Rice:

Jollof rice is a popular West African dish that features a flavorful blend of rice, tomatoes, onions, and various vegetables. While the exact recipe can vary by region, jollof rice is typically prepared by first sautéing onions and other aromatic vegetables like bell peppers and garlic. Then, tomato paste, spices, and stock are added to create a rich base. Finally, rice and vegetables such as carrots, peas, and green beans are added and cooked until tender. Jollof rice can be enjoyed as a standalone dish or paired with grilled or stewed meats for a complete and satisfying meal.

2. Egusi Soup:

Egusi soup is a staple in Nigerian cuisine and showcases the versatility of African vegetables. This hearty soup is made from ground melon seeds (egusi) and typically includes a variety of vegetables such as spinach, bitter leaf, pumpkin leaves, and okra. The melon seeds are ground and used as a thickening agent, creating a creamy and flavorful base. The vegetables are then added along with spices and protein such as fish, meat, or shrimp, resulting in a nutritious and delicious soup that can be enjoyed with fufu (a starchy staple) or rice.

3. Sukuma Wiki:

Sukuma wiki, which translates to "stretch the week" in Swahili, is a popular Kenyan dish. It is primarily made with collard greens, tomatoes, onions, and spices. The dish gets its name from its affordability and ability to "stretch" a meal throughout the week. Sukuma wiki is often stir-fried with onions and tomatoes until the greens wilt down and become tender. This simple yet flavorsome side dish pairs well with Ugali (a cornmeal porridge) or Chapatis (flaky flatbreads). It is a nutritious and affordable dish that is enjoyed by many in East Africa.

4. Bobotie:

Bobotie is a traditional South African dish that combines meat, spices, and vegetables to create a mouthwatering meal. It is typically made with minced lamb or beef, onions, garlic, curry powder, and various dried fruits like raisins or apricots. Grated carrots and chopped tomatoes are also added to enhance the flavors and provide a satisfying texture. The mixture is then baked until golden and served with sides such as yellow rice, chutney, and vegetables. Bobotie is a unique fusion of African, Malay, and Dutch flavors, making it a true representation of South African cuisine.

FROM THE AROMATIC SPICES of West Africa to the leafy greens of East Africa, African cuisine offers a vibrant array of vegetable-based dishes. Whether it's the rich flavors of jollof rice, the creamy texture of egusi soup, the simplicity of sukuma wiki, or the fusion of flavors in bobotie, African vegetables are showcased in a variety of delicious recipes. Exploring the world of African cuisine not only opens up a whole new world of flavors but also highlights the importance of vegetables in African culinary traditions. So, next time you're feeling adventurous in the kitchen, consider trying out these examples and recipes to discover the wonders of African vegetable-based dishes.

Chapter 12: The Dairy of African Cuisine- The cheese and butter that flavor African cuisine

Chapter 12: The Diary of African Cuisine- The Cheese and Butter that Flavor African Cuisine

IN THE VAST LANDSCAPE of African cuisine, one cannot overlook the importance of dairy products in enhancing flavors and enriching traditional dishes. From the rolling savannahs of East Africa to the bustling markets of West Africa, cheese and butter have carved a niche for themselves in the culinary traditions of the continent. In this chapter, we explore the fascinating journey of these dairy delights and how they have become an integral part of Africa's rich gastronomic tapestry.

The Origins:

Cheese and butter, while not originally indigenous to Africa, have been adopted and adapted by its diverse cultures over the centuries. Historical records suggest that the presence of dairy in Africa can be traced back to ancient Egyptian civilizations, where it was primarily used for medicinal purposes.

As trade routes expanded and interactions between different communities flourished, the art of cheesemaking began to spread. Arab and European merchants introduced various cheese and butter-making techniques to the continent, further fueling the evolution of Africa's dairy traditions.

A Taste of Diversity:

Africa's history of colonization and cultural diffusion is reflected in the vast assortment of cheeses and butters that exist today. From mild and crumbly to pungent and aged, African cheese comes in an awe-inspiring variety.

One of the most renowned African cheeses is feta-like briddies, which originates from South Africa. Made from goat's milk, it possesses a distinctive tangy and salty flavor. In Nigeria, those who enjoy strong flavors turn to Wura cheese, a piquant variety made from cow's or goat's milk and traditionally aged for months.

In terms of butter, Niter Kibbeh serves as Ethiopia's prime example. Often referred to as spiced butter, it is meticulously prepared by clarifying the milk solids, then simmering a blend of aromatic spices and herbs with the clarified butter. The result is a tantalizingly rich buttery flavor with hints of ginger, cloves, and cardamom.

Infusing Flavor into African Dishes:

Cheese and butter delightfully enhance the flavors and textures of various African dishes. For instance, Mozambique's Matapane, a traditional cornmeal porridge, is made even more indulgent with a generous dollop of butter, which melts into the creamy mixture. Similarly, in Ghana, the renowned dish, Waakye, combines rice and beans with grated cheese for a scrumptious twist.

African chefs also often incorporate specialized cheeses into classic dishes. Moroccan pastilla, a sweet and savory pie filled with spiced meat, almonds, and topped with powdered sugar, exhibits a sublime contrast when made with creamy goat cheese rather than traditional chicken. Likewise, a popular West African vegetable soup called Muganzaflav is taken to another level when garnished with crumbled khoa cheese, lending a distinctive richness to the dish.

Reviving Traditional Practices:

In recent years, there has been a growing movement across Africa to rediscover and revive traditional cheesemaking and butter churn techniques. Small-scale artisanal producers are once again turning to decentralized methods, using locally sourced milk and preserving regional flavor profiles.

This revival not only highlights the importance of preserving culinary legacy but also creates economic opportunities for local communities. By coupling traditional dairy practices with modern safety and quality standards, artisan cheesemakers and butter producers are carving a niche for themselves in a world dominated by industrialized dairy giants.

THE INCLUSION OF CHEESE and butter in African cuisine is a testament to the continent's ability to embrace and celebrate new culinary influences while staying true to its roots. Through centuries of historical exchange, African cheese and butter have become a vibrant and indispensable part of the continent's culinary identity. As artisans and chefs continue to experiment with various flavors and techniques, we can look forward to a future where Africa's dairy delights continue to captivate taste buds around the world.

- The milk and yogurt that refresh African cuisine

Milk and yogurt are refreshingly delicious dairy products that have become an essential part of African cuisine. They are not only loved for their taste but also for their incredible nutritional value and versatility in cooking. From classic African dishes to modern culinary innovations, milk and yogurt play a significant role in elevating the flavors and textures found in African cuisine.

In many African countries, milk is traditionally sourced from cows, goats, and camels, while yogurt is often prepared using fermented cow's milk. The methods of milk production and yogurt-making have been passed down through generations, resulting in time-honored techniques that are still widely practiced today.

Milk, with its rich and creamy texture, is a common ingredient in various traditional African dishes. It adds depth and richness to soups and stews, such as the famous Nigerian Egusi soup or the savory South African Bobotie. In East Africa, milk is a key component in staples like Ugali, a thick maize porridge, and Wali wa Nazi, a coconut-flavored rice dish.

Aside from its culinary uses, milk is cherished in African cultures for its symbolic value. It is often used in traditional rituals and celebrations as an offering to deities and ancestral spirits, symbolizing fertility and abundant blessings. This reverence for milk showcases its integral role in African society and its significance to the people's cultural heritage.

Yogurt, on the other hand, adds a tangy and creamy twist to both sweet and savory recipes in African cuisine. It can be enjoyed as a refreshing standalone snack or incorporated into inventive dishes. In Ethiopia, Dabo Kolo, a spiced, crunchy snack, is made by mixing yogurt with finely ground grains and spices and frying them to crisp perfection. In Somalia, a popular sweet treat called Masago Cheel, made with a combination of yogurt, sugar, and fresh fruit, is served during festive occasions.

One notable characteristic of yogurt in African cuisine is the art of fermentation, resulting in a tangy yet mild flavor. Fermented yogurt contains probiotics, which offer numerous health benefits, including aiding digestion and bolstering the immune system. This healthy aspect of yogurt has caught the attention of health-conscious individuals worldwide, contributing to the growing popularity of African-inspired yogurt variations internationally.

In recent years, African chefs and food entrepreneurs have been reimagining milk and yogurt in modern culinary settings. They have taken traditional recipes and introduced unique flavor combinations and innovative presentations, catering to a wider audience and further highlighting the diverse flavors of African cuisine.

In conclusion, milk and yogurt add a delightful and nutritious dimension to African cuisine, be it in traditional dishes or modern culinary creations. With their versatility, symbolic value, and cultural significance, they have become important ingredients that refresh and enhance the flavors of African meals. So, whether you are exploring the diverse tastes of Africa or incorporating new flavors into your own cooking, don't forget to embrace the milk and yogurt that play an integral role in this rich and exciting culinary tradition.

- The examples and recipes of dishes that showcase the dairy of African cuisine

African cuisine is known for its unique flavors and vibrant culinary traditions. From mouth-watering stews to delectable desserts, there is a wide variety of dishes that showcase the richness of dairy in African cooking. In this article, we will explore some examples and recipes of African dishes that make use of dairy products.

1. Cachupa – Cape Verdean Style

Cachupa is a popular dish in Cape Verde, a country off the coast of West Africa. It is a hearty stew made with various ingredients such as corn, beans, vegetables, and meat or fish. To add creaminess and richness to this dish, coconut milk is often used. This dairy alternative gives cachupa a wonderful flavor and luxurious texture.

Recipe:

- In a large pot, combine diced onions, garlic, and oil. Sauté until the onions are translucent.

- Add diced potatoes, carrots, pumpkin, and water. Simmer until the vegetables are partially cooked.

- Stir in corn kernels, kidney beans, diced ham, and/or chunks of fish. Cook until the meat is tender.

- Pour in coconut milk and season with salt, pepper, and other desired spices.

- Simmer the stew for another 15-20 minutes, allowing the flavors to meld together.

- Serve cachupa hot with a side of rice or bread.

2. Bobotie – South African Delight

Bobotie is a traditional South African dish that originated from the Cape Malay community. It is a baked minced meat dish with an egg-based topping. To give the dish a creamy and indulgent twist, a mixture of milk or yogurt, eggs, and spices is poured over the meat before baking. The resulting bobotie is aromatic and delicious, with a golden crust and a creamy layer beneath.

Recipe:

- In a skillet, sauté ground beef or lamb with onions, garlic, and curry powder until the meat is browned.

- Add raisins, chutney, almonds, and breadcrumbs soaked in milk. Mix well.

- Transfer the meat mixture into a greased baking dish.

- In a separate bowl, whisk together milk or yogurt, eggs, salt, and pepper. Pour this mixture over the meat.

- Bake in a preheated oven at 180°C (350°F) for 25-30 minutes until the top is lightly browned.

- Allow bobotie to cool for a few minutes before serving. It pairs well with yellow rice and roasted vegetables.

3. Kisra – Sudanese Flatbread

Kisra is a traditional Sudanese flatbread made from sorghum flour. It is a staple in Sudanese cuisine and is often eaten with stews such as daraba (lamb stew) or mullah (okra stew). To give kisra a softer and more velvety texture, many Sudanese households add a touch of fermented milk known as "sig" or "jibna." This dairy product adds a unique tanginess and complements the flavor of the bread.

Recipe:

- In a mixing bowl, combine sorghum flour, water, and salt. Stir until you have a smooth batter.

- Cover the bowl and let the batter ferment overnight, allowing it to develop a slightly sour taste.

- Preheat a non-stick pan or griddle over medium heat.

- Pour a ladleful of batter onto the pan and spread it into a large, thin circle.

- Cook the kisra until it begins to bubble and the edges appear crispy. Flip it over and cook for another minute or two.

- Repeat with the remaining batter.

- Serve kisra warm, either on its own or with your favorite stews.

African cuisine offers a plethora of flavors and techniques that incorporate dairy products in delicious and unexpected ways. Whether it's the creamy coconut milk in cachupa, the custard-like topping of bobotie, or the tangy fermented milk in kisra, these examples and recipes demonstrate the diversity and creativity found in dairy-infused African dishes. So, embark on a flavorful culinary journey and explore the myriad of dairy delights that African cuisine has to offer!

Chapter 13: The Breads of African Cuisine-The flatbreads and pastries that accompany African cuisine

Across the vast continent of Africa, bread holds a special place in the hearts and kitchens of its people. From the deserts of North Africa to the lush green landscapes of sub-Saharan Africa, breads and pastries serve as essential accompaniments to African cuisine. This chapter delves into the world of African flatbreads and pastries, uncovering their rich history, diverse flavors, and techniques.

1. Exploration of African Flatbreads:

1.1 Ethiopian Injera: A staple of Ethiopian cuisine, injera is a tangy, spongy flatbread made from the indigenous cereal known as teff. We explore the art of making injera, including the crucial fermentation process that lends it its distinctive flavor.

1.2 South African Vetkoek: Vetkoek, meaning "fat cake" in Afrikaans, is a beloved snack in South Africa. This versatile bread is deep-fried and can be stuffed with various savory or sweet fillings. We unravel the secrets to making perfectly golden vetkoek.

1.3 Chapati from East Africa: Known by different names across the continent, chapati is a flaky flatbread commonly enjoyed in East Africa. We delve into the technique of rolling and frying these delectable bread discs, and how they have become inseparable from African mealtime.

2. Diving into African Pastry Traditions:

2.1 North African Msemen: Msemen, a Moroccan delicacy, is a must-taste for any pastry enthusiast. This luscious square-shaped pastry is made from layered and fried dough, resulting in a buttery and tender treat. We unveil the various ways in which msemen is served in different regions of North Africa.

2.2 Malawi Mandazi: In Malawi, mandazi holds a special place on breakfast tables. These fluffy, deep-fried dumplings offer a delightful complement to African tea or coffee. We explore the diverse twists and variations of mandazi recipes passed down through generations.

2.3 Nigerian Puff Puff: As one of the most popular street foods in Nigeria, puff puff has gained fame beyond the continent's borders. These doughy balls delight with their airy texture and limitless flavor alterations. We showcase the art of creating the perfect puff puff, enjoyed nationwide.

3. The Influence of African Breads on Global Cuisine:

3.1 The Diaspora Impact: African flatbreads and pastries have made their way into global culinary scenes through the diaspora. We navigate through the African influence on Caribbean breads like Johnny Cakes and bakes, shedding light on the cultural connections that have shaped these recipes.

3.2 Fusion with Western Cuisine: African breads and pastry techniques have also merged with Western baking traditions, resulting in flavorful fusions. We explore examples such as Tunisian-style pizza, highlighting how these culinary exchanges have enriched both continents' cuisines.

AFRICAN BREADS AND pastries offer a kaleidoscope of flavors, shapes, and traditions. Through the exploration of injera, vetkoek, chapati, msemen, mandazi, puff puff, and their global influences, we dive into the rich world of African baked goods. Whether enjoyed alongside hearty stews, used as edible utensils, or relished as a solitary pleasure, the breads of African cuisine embody the legacy, creativity, and culinary wealth of the continent.

- The leavened and unleavened breads that vary African cuisine

African cuisine is incredibly diverse, with each region incorporating its own unique flavors, ingredients, and cooking techniques. One aspect that plays a significant role in African cooking is bread, which holds great cultural and culinary importance for various communities across the continent. Among the different types of bread in African cuisine, two prevalent categories are leavened and unleavened breads.

Leavened bread, also known as risen bread, is a type of bread that uses yeast or other leavening agents to make the dough rise and create a soft, fluffy texture. In African cuisine, leavened bread is often made using a mixture of flour, water, salt, and yeast. This dough is left to rest and ferment, allowing the yeast to release carbon dioxide, causing the dough to rise.

Leavened bread holds significant cultural importance in several African countries. In Ethiopia, injera is a popular example of a fermented flatbread that is made from teff flour. This sourdough-like bread requires no added yeast but is naturally fermented for several days, resulting in a tangy and slightly spongy texture. Injera is not only a staple in Ethiopian cuisine but is also used as a utensil to scoop up stews and other dishes.

Similarly, in Sudan and Egypt, different varieties of fermented breads are consumed, such as kesra and aish baladi, respectively. These breads are often enjoyed alongside traditional dishes such as ful medames or molokhia and are a common sight on the dining table.

On the other hand, unleavened bread, also known as flatbread, is made without yeast or another raising agent. Typically, unleavened bread is made by combining flour, water, and salt, and then rolling out the dough into thin sheets. It is then cooked over direct heat, either on a griddle, in the oven, or even on an open flame.

Unleavened bread is popular in various regions of Africa. In West Africa, for example, the region's most famous flatbread is fufu. It is made from pounded cassava or yam flour and often eaten with soups, stews or sauces. Fufu is particularly cherished in countries such as Nigeria and Ghana, where it is a staple food.

Similarly, in North Africa, especially in countries like Morocco and Algeria, a flatbread known as khobz is prominently consumed. Khobz is a round, unleavened bread that is typically made with semolina flour and enjoyed with various dishes throughout the day.

Both leavened and unleavened breads contribute to the diverse and vibrant tapestry of African cuisine. From the sourdough-like injera to the thin and flexible fufu or khobz, these types of bread highlight the culinary creativity and distinct cultural practices found throughout Africa. Whether consumed plain, as an accompaniment to other dishes, or used as an edible utensil, bread in its many forms plays an essential role in African cuisine, serving as a delicious cornerstone of various meals rooted in tradition and identity.

- The examples and recipes of dishes that showcase the breads of African cuisine

One of the defining features of African cuisine is the incredible variety of breads that are part of its gastronomic heritage. From the light and fluffy injera of Ethiopia to the hearty and dense ngiri of Zimbabwe, African breads showcase a multitude of flavors, textures, and ingredients. In this article, we will explore some examples and recipes of dishes that proudly put these breads at the forefront.

Injera, arguably the most famous African bread, is a staple in Ethiopian and Eritrean cuisine. This flat, spongy bread, made from fermented teff flour, has a distinct tangy flavor that perfectly complements the rich and aromatic stews typically served with it. Injera is traditionally cooked on a large clay or cast-iron pan called a mitad, which gives it a unique shape and characteristic appearance. To make injera at home, mix teff flour with water and allow it to ferment for at least 12 hours. Cook small ladlefuls of the batter on a non-stick pan, swirling it around to create a thin, pancake-like bread. Once the edges start to curl and the top is no longer wet, remove the injera from the pan and stack them on top of each other to keep them soft and pliable. Serve injera alongside dishes like doro wat (spicy chicken stew) or miser wat (red lentil stew) for an authentic Ethiopian experience.

Moving westward to Nigeria, we encounter masa, a delicious bread made from fermented rice batter. Masa is commonly eaten for breakfast or as a light snack, especially during festive occasions. To make masa, soak rice overnight and grind it into a smooth batter the next day. Allow the batter to ferment for a few hours and then cook small portions in a greased pan, similar to how pancakes are made. The resulting bread is a soft, slightly tangy delight that pairs beautifully with a variety of toppings. Try serving masa with potato and vegetable stir-fry known as yam sauce or dip it in a rich tomato-based stew for a heartier meal.

Venturing to the southern region of Africa, we come across the ngiri bread of Zimbabwe. Ngiri, also known as sadza, is a dense, unleavened cornmeal bread that is cooked to perfection. It is a staple food in Zimbabwean cuisine and is often served with a selection of relishes or stews. To make ngiri, bring water to a boil and gradually stir in cornmeal until a thick, stiff porridge is formed. Allow it to cool and then shape it into flat rounds or small balls. Cook the ngiri on a griddle until golden brown and perfectly crisp. The resulting bread has a deliciously nutty flavor and provides a wonderful contrast to the flavorful accompaniments it is served with, such as beef stew or vegetable curry.

These are just a few examples of African breads and the delightful dishes that showcase them. Each region and country on the continent has its own unique bread varieties, each with its own distinct processes, flavors, and textures. Incorporating these breads into your cooking repertoire will not only introduce you to new flavors but also offer a glimpse of the rich culinary heritage of Africa.

Chapter 14: The Sweets of African Cuisine- The cakes and cookies that delight African cuisine

African cuisine is renowned for its rich and diverse array of flavors, but when it comes to satisfying one's sweet tooth, the continent also offers some delectable delights in the form of cakes and cookies. In this chapter, we will delve into the world of African sweet treats, exploring their unique ingredients, preparation methods, and the cultural significance they hold. From West African peanut cookies to East African coconut cakes, get ready to tantalize your taste buds with an exploration of the sweet side of African cuisine.

Section 1: The Land of Diversity- Varieties of African Desserts

Africa is a vast continent with diverse culinary traditions, and its desserts are no exception. Different regions boast specific sweet treats that reflect their local ingredients and cultural influences. From the golden brown Sooji Ladoo of North Africa, made with semolina, ghee, and cardamom, to the rich and decadent Rooibos Chocolate Tarts of Southern Africa, African cakes and cookies showcase a marvelous tapestry of flavors and textures.

Section 2: Traditional Ingredients and Flavors

African desserts incorporate a wide range of traditional ingredients that result in unique and tantalizing flavors. For instance, in West Africa, where groundnuts are abundant, peanut-infused cakes, such as the Senegalese peanut cake, become a staple. In East Africa, coconut features prominently in desserts like the Tanzanian coconut mandazi, a deep-fried bread similar to a doughnut, with a fragrant coconutty twist.

Section 3: Cultural Significance- Celebrations and Sweet Treats

In African culture, food is often a symbol of celebration and togetherness. Cakes and cookies hold a special place in traditional festivities, where they are shared among friends and family during joyous occasions. By exploring these desserts, we can gain insight into the cultural significance attached to these delightful treats, whether it's the rich symbolism of the Nigerian puff puff served during weddings, or the Kanyonga cookies baked in Zambia to celebrate the end of the harvest season.

Section 4: Fusion and Contemporary Twists

African desserts continue to evolve, influenced by a variety of culinary exchanges and contemporary tastes. Talented chefs and home cooks are increasingly experimenting with fusion desserts and incorporating global ingredients and inspirations. This section showcases modern twists on African sweet treats, such as the Moroccan spiced orange cake infused with cardamom and saffron, or the Ghanaian chocolate tarts with a hint of chili for a delightful kick.

Conclusion

As we conclude our exploration of African sweet treats, it becomes evident that the cakes and cookies of African cuisine are not only tantalizing for the taste buds but also showcases the continent's rich diversity, heritage, and culinary imagination. From the familiar to the exotic, these delights offer a glimpse into African culture, history, and celebration through their mouthwatering flavors. Let us embrace the sweetness of African cuisine, one bite at a time.

Epilogue

African desserts are a treasure trove waiting to be discovered and appreciated. The unique combination of indigenous ingredients, innovative techniques, and cultural significance make these cakes and cookies a true representation of Africa's culinary prowess. So, the next time you have a craving for something sweet, take a journey to the heart of Africa and indulge in the delectable offerings of its dessert landscape.

- The puddings and custards that comfort African cuisine

Puddings and custards have long been cherished as comforting and indulgent desserts in various cuisines around the world. In African cuisine, these delectable treats hold a special place, offering a delightful end to a hearty meal. From rich and creamy textures to the use of unique flavors and ingredients, African puddings and custards showcase the diversity and complexity of the continent's culinary traditions.

One of the most iconic African puddings is Malva pudding. Hailing from South Africa, this decadent dessert is made with a generous amount of apricot jam, which gives it a velvety texture and a pleasant tangy flavor. It is traditionally served warm and drenched in a sticky caramel sauce, creating a lusciously sweet concoction that melts in the mouth. This comforting dish epitomizes home-cooked goodness and is a favorite for celebrations and gatherings.

Moving towards West Africa, you will find Moin Moin, a pudding-like dish made from black-eyed peas. Moin Moin is a staple in Nigerian cuisine and is often served as a side dish or eaten as a snack. The black-eyed peas are ground into a smooth paste, seasoned with onions, peppers, and spices, and wrapped in banana leaves or aluminum foil before being steamed or baked. The result is a dense custard-like texture with a subtle smoky flavor that pairs well with stews or rice dishes.

In East Africa, a well-liked pudding is Mandazi – sweet fried donuts often referred to as Swahili beignets. These golden goodies are a popular street food snack, and their sweet, doughy flavor instantly brings comfort and joy. Mandazi is frequently flavored with coconut milk, cardamom, and cinnamon, infusing the dessert with a fragrant and aromatic quality. Sprinkled with powdered sugar or served with a dipping sauce made from condensed milk, these treats provide a delightful sugar rush.

Heading further north, Egypt showcases its version of a classic pudding called Mahalabiya. This silky treat is made from almond milk boiled with sugar and flavored with rosewater and orange blossom water. The pudding is thickened with cornstarch, creating a smooth and creamy consistency that is perfectly balanced with the floral scents. Once chilled and set, Mahalabiya is often garnished with crushed pistachios or desiccated coconut, adding a touch of crunch to the velvety creation.

The diversity and richness of African pudding and custard recipes reflect the continent's eclectic culinary heritage and regional variations. While some highlight local ingredients like black-eyed peas or apricot jam, others fuse traditional flavors with international influences. What remains constant, however, is their comforting nature. A bite of any African pudding or custard is sure to bring warm nostalgia and a sense of belonging, making these desserts an integral part of African cuisine.

- The examples and recipes of dishes that showcase the sweets of African cuisine

One cannot speak of African cuisine without acknowledging its delectable array of sweets. From mouthwatering desserts to unique pastries, African sweets boast a rich diversity that reflects the continent's vibrant culture and history. In this article, we will explore some tantalizing examples and recipes of dishes that showcase the sweets of African cuisine.

1. Koeksisters- South Africa:

Originating from the Cape Malay community in South Africa, koeksisters are one of the most beloved desserts in the country. These deep-fried pastries are soaked in a sticky syrup, resulting in a sweet, sticky, and indulgent treat. To make koeksisters, start by mixing flour, butter, sugar, and baking powder to form a dough. Cut the dough into strips, then fry them until golden brown. Once fried, the koeksisters are immediately dipped in ice-cold syrup made with sugar, water, and lemon juice. The syrup soaks into the pastries, creating a delightful combination of textures and flavors.

2. Mandazi- East Africa:

Mandazi, also known as Swahili donuts, are a popular sweet treat in East Africa, particularly in Kenya and Tanzania. These fluffy, deep-fried pastries are often enjoyed as a snack or combined with a cup of spiced tea. To make mandazi, combine flour, sugar, yeast, cardamom, and nutmeg in a large bowl. Gradually add warm water and knead the dough until smooth. Let it rise for a while before rolling it out and cutting it into triangular or square shapes. Deep-fry the mandazi until golden brown and sprinkle them with powdered sugar. The result is a light, aromatic pastry that satisfies any sweet tooth.

3. Atayef- Middle East/North Africa:

While not exclusively African, atayef is commonly found in North African countries and is a popular Ramadan dessert. These small, folded pancakes are filled with a mixture of sweetened cheese or nuts. To make atayef, combine flour, yeast, sugar, and water to create a batter. Allow the mixture to rest for around 30 minutes, then pour small circles of batter onto a hot griddle or non-stick pan. Once the surface is bubbly and dry, remove the pancakes and set them aside to cool. Fill each pancake with a small spoonful of either sweetened cheese or crushed nuts, fold them into crescents, and seal the edges with a bit of water. Fry the atayef until lightly browned, and serve them drizzled with honey or sugar syrup for an exquisite dessert experience.

4. Mbatata Cake- Mozambique:

Mbatata cake, also known as Mozambican sweet potato cake, showcases the unique flavors and ingredients of African sweets. This rich cake is made with sweet potatoes, giving it a naturally sweet and moist texture. Additionally, the balance of spices and flavors adds a distinct twist to the dessert. To make mbatata cake, start by boiling and mashing sweet potatoes. Mix them with butter, sugar, eggs, flour, grated coconut, lemon zest, and spices like cinnamon, nutmeg, and cloves. Bake the batter in a greased cake pan until a toothpick inserted into the center comes out clean. The result is a delightful, aromatic cake that wonderfully blends sweet and savory flavors.

As we've seen, African sweets offer a delightful journey through a wide range of flavors, ingredients, and cooking techniques. Whether you're savoring traditional South African pastries or enjoying the aromatic spices of North African desserts, exploring the sweets of African cuisine is sure to please any palate.

Chapter 15: The Drinks of African Cuisine- The teas and coffees that energize African cuisine

In African cuisine, there are various beverages that not only quench thirst but also provide a burst of energy and rejuvenation. Teas and coffees play an integral role in African culture, offering a rich flavorsome experience that invigorates and revitalizes the body and mind. Let's explore the diverse range of teas and coffees that grace African cuisine and make it a uniquely aromatic and uplifting culinary journey.

1. Tea Blends:

African tea blends are a fusion of indigenous plants and exotic spices, creating a harmonious balance between health benefits and taste. One renowned tea blend is the Moroccan Mint Tea. Combining green tea, fresh mint leaves, and sugar, this refreshing drink is a staple in North Africa, enjoyed brewed hot or served over ice with a sprig of mint. The Rooibos tea, originating from South Africa, is another notable inclusion. Its caffeine-free nature and unique earthy flavors make it a popular choice for both health-conscious individuals and tea enthusiasts.

2. Ethiopian Coffee:

Ethiopia, often hailed as the birthplace of coffee, offers a truly enriching coffee experience. Coffee is deeply ingrained in Ethiopian culture, with elaborate coffee ceremonies being an essential part of social gatherings. Ethiopian coffee is known for its complex flavors and intensity. Traditionally roasted on an open flame and then freshly ground, the coffee is brewed in a clay pot called a jebena. This process harnesses the rich aromas and creates a cup of coffee that is both intense and invigorating.

3. South African Red Bush Tea:

Another exceptional tea that graces African cuisine is the South African Rooibos, also known as Red Bush Tea. This caffeine-free tea is brimming with health benefits and is celebrated for its distinct reddish hue and sweet undertones. Packed with antioxidants and minerals, this herbal infusion is known for its ability to aid digestion, soothe allergies, and promote relaxation, making it a popular choice for those seeking a caffeine-free alternative.

4. Sahara Desert Tea:

In North Africa, particularly Libya and Algeria, a quintessential drink known as Sahara Desert Tea is prepared by steeping an array of herbs and spices such as sage, mint, and wormwood in boiling water. This concoction is then served with a generous amount of sugar, creating a uniquely sweet and aromatic tea that energizes and uplifts, especially in the scorching heat of the desert.

5. Senegal Bissap:

Senegal, known for its vibrant cuisine, brings Bissap to the table, a thirst-quenching hibiscus tea. Made by steeping dried hibiscus petals with sugar and various aromatic spices, Bissap delivers a delightful balance of tart and sweet flavors. Traditionally served chilled, this crimson-colored drink is not only refreshing but also provides a multitude of health benefits, including improved digestion and blood pressure regulation.

TEAS AND COFFEES IN African cuisine exemplify the careful balance between flavor and functional benefits. From Moroccan Mint Tea to Ethiopian Coffee, each cup transports individuals on a sensory journey, invigorating their taste buds and providing an energizing boost. Whether maintaining cultural traditions or seeking new taste experiences, African teas and coffees offer a delightful array of options for those in search of aromatic and revitalizing beverages. So, indulge in the distinctive world of African beverages, and enjoy the invigorating flavors that accompany this rich and diverse cuisine.

- The beers and wines that celebrate African cuisine

In recent years, there has been a surge in interest and appreciation for African cuisine. Inspired by the bold flavors, rich history, and diverse cultures of the continent, restaurateurs, chefs, and home cooks have begun showcasing the delicious dishes from Africa's many regions. And where there is incredible food, there also must be alcohol to complement it. That is where the beers and wines celebrating African cuisine come in.

Beer plays a significant role in African culinary traditions, with different countries boasting their unique brewing techniques and styles. One notable beer that celebrates African cuisine is the South African ale known as Umqombothi. Dating back centuries, this traditional home-brewed beer is made from maize, sorghum, water, and yeast. Umqombothi is enjoyed during traditional ceremonies and social gatherings, offering a real taste of South African heritage.

Moving to East Africa, we find the Tusker lager from Kenya. This iconic brew is a testament to the Kenyan heritage and culture. Tusker is known for its crisp and refreshing taste, making it an ideal match for African dishes that feature bold spices and unique flavors. The balance between the beer's bitterness and the food's intensity creates a harmonious pairing that is a delight for the taste buds.

Continuing on our culinary journey, we arrive in Ethiopia, home to the popular fermented drink called Tej. Tej is a honey wine, with a history that goes back to ancient times. It is made from a mix of honey, water, and gesho leaves. Tej has a similar concept to mead, with a slightly sweet taste and a distinct floral aroma derived from the gesho leaves. This traditional Ethiopian drink is often enjoyed during festive occasions and pairs well with their spicy and aromatic dishes such as Doro Wat or Kitfo.

Another remarkable wine that celebrates African cuisine is Amarula Cream Liqueur from South Africa. Made from the exotic fruit called Marula, this cream liqueur incorporates the unique flavors of the African continent. Known for its rich and creamy texture, Amarula offers a smooth and velvety experience with hints of caramel and exotic fruit. With its luxurious taste, it can be comfortably sipped on its own or added to various cocktails. Pairing Amarula with African-inspired desserts or serving it as a chilled after-dinner drink is a great way to indulge in the flavors of Africa.

As interest in African cuisine continues to grow, so does the variety of beers and wines created to honor this rich culinary tradition. By embracing these beverages, we can create an immersive experience that truly celebrates the African flavors and the continent's vibrant culinary heritage. So go ahead, grab a bottle of Umqombothi, Tusker, Tej, or Amarula, and embark on a tantalizing journey through the sumptuous world of African cuisine.

- The examples and recipes of drinks that showcase the drinks of African cuisine

Flavors of Africa: Examples and Recipes of Drinks Showcasing African Cuisine

AFRICAN CUISINE IS renowned for its rich and diverse flavors, which extend beyond just food to the refreshing and tantalizing world of beverages. This article serves as a guide to explore the richness and excellence of African drinks. We will delve into a myriad of examples and recipes, highlighting some of the most fascinating and iconic beverages that can be found throughout the continent.

1. Hibiscus Flavored Drinks:

One of the most well-known and beloved African drinks is undoubtedly the Hibiscus-infused beverage, commonly known as "Bissap" or "Sobolo." Made by steeping dried hibiscus petals in hot water and sweetening it with sugar or honey, this vibrant and tangy drink is refreshing, especially when served iced. It's a ubiquitous drink, enjoyed throughout African countries such as Nigeria (Zobo), Egypt (Karkade), and Senegal (Bissap).

Recipe- Bissap:
– 2 cups dried hibiscus petals
– 8 cups water
– 1 cup sugar
– 1 tbsp grated ginger (optional)
– Juice of 2-3 limes
Method:
1. Boil the water in a pot and add the dried hibiscus petals. Steep for about 20 minutes.
2. Strain the petals from the liquid and pour it back into the pot.
3. Add sugar and ginger (if desired), then bring it to a boil.
4. Remove from heat and let it cool before squeezing the lime juice.

5. Serve chilled, preferably with ice cubes.

2. Palm Wine:

Palm wine, a traditional African drink, holds cultural significance in many countries of West and Central Africa. It is obtained from the sap of various palm trees, primarily the oil palm or the raffia palm. This sweet, fermented concoction can be enjoyed in its mild, non-alcoholic form or left to further ferment, creating a subtly fermented alcoholic beverage.

Recipe- Raffia Palm Wine:

– Fresh sap from raffia palm tree

Method:

1. Climb a mature raffia palm tree and collect the sap from the cut flowers or natural spouts.

2. Pour the sap into a fermented clay pot or an airtight container.

3. Place it in a cool, dark place and let it ferment for a few hours for the non-alcoholic version or up to 24 hours for alcoholic palm wine.

4. Serve chilled in traditionally carved calabash or any other desired beverage serving containers.

3. Ginger Beer:

African ginger beer is a fiery and invigorating drink, popular primarily in Southern and East African countries like South Africa, Zimbabwe, and Tanzania. Its intense ginger taste combined with sugar and lemon or lime juice makes it a zesty delight.

Recipe- Ginger Beer:

– 1 large piece of ginger (about 2 inches)

– Juice of 4 lemons or limes

– 1 cup sugar

– 5 cups water

– ¼ teaspoon instant yeast

– Ice cubes (to serve)

Method:

1. Peel and grate the ginger, then place it in a bowl.

2. Add lemon/lime juice and sugar, mix well until sugar dissolves.

3. Boil the water and pour it over the ginger mixture. Let it steep for an hour.

4. Strain the liquid, capturing the gingery syrup.

5. Dissolve the yeast in ¼ cup of water, then mix it with the ginger syrup.

6. Bottle the mixture in airtight containers or bottles leaving some headspace for fermentation.

7. Leave it at room temperature for 24-48 hours, then refrigerate.

8. Serve chilled over ice cubes.

THE FLAVORS OF AFRICAN drinks truly embody the diversity and essence of the African continent. From the tangy hibiscus-infused beverages to the naturally fermented palm wine and the zesty kick of ginger beer, African beverages are a true reflection of regional traditions, cultural heritage, and pure refreshment. Indulging in these unique African drinks is not only a delight for the taste buds but also a journey into the vibrant culinary tapestry that Africa offers.

Chapter 16: The Breakfasts of African Cuisine- The importance and variety of breakfasts in African cuisine

Breakfast is often considered the most important meal of the day, and this rings true in African cuisine as well. African breakfasts are diverse and offer a range of flavors, ingredients, and preparation methods that are unique to each region and country. In this chapter, we will explore the significance and variety of breakfasts in African cuisine, highlighting the rich culinary traditions that have shaped these morning meals.

1. The significance of breakfast in African culture:

Breakfast in African culture is more than just a meal. It serves as a time for nourishment, community, and starting the day with energy and vitality. The ingredients used in African breakfasts are typically sourced locally, reflecting the connection to the land and the community. Breakfast is also a valuable occasion for family members to gather, share stories, and bond before engaging in daily activities.

2. Staple Ingredients:

Across Africa, several staple ingredients are commonly featured in breakfast dishes. Some include millet, cornmeal, yam, plantains, sorghum, beans, and various fruits. These ingredients provide carbohydrate-rich meals that offer sustenance and energy for the day ahead.

3. West African Breakfasts:

In West Africa, breakfasts often feature dishes such as Akara, which are deep-fried bean cakes, or Moin Moin, a steamed bean pudding. These protein-rich breakfasts are often enjoyed with staples like cornmeal porridge or moi moi bread. Additionally, a popular breakfast beverage is Kunu, a millet or sorghum-based drink enjoyed hot or cold.

4. East African Breakfasts:

East African breakfasts are diverse, reflecting the region's cultural and culinary influences. In countries like Kenya, Ugali, a cornmeal-based dish, is commonly served with sukuma wiki (collard greens) and meat stew. In

Ethiopia, a traditional breakfast consists of injera, a fermented pancake-like bread, served with a variety of stews and sauces known as wat. Other popular breakfasts in the region include mandazi, similar to a donut, and chai tea, spiced and sweetened with milk.

5. North African Breakfasts:

North African countries offer breakfast dishes with a Mediterranean influence, blended with indigenous flavors. A famous example is Morocco's traditional breakfast, featuring msemen, a flaky semolina pancake, served along with honey, cheese, and a variety of olives. Another well-known breakfast option is Shakshuka, a tomato and egg dish cooked with spices such as cumin and paprika.

6. Southern African Breakfasts:

Breakfasts in Southern Africa showcase a fusion of culinary traditions from indigenous communities and European settlers. Porridge made from mealie meal (cornmeal), known as pap or phutu, is a popular breakfast dish, often served with tomato and onion sauces or chakalaka, a spicy vegetable relish. Biltong (dried cured meat), eggs, and baked goods like the soetkoekie (a sweet biscuit) are also commonly enjoyed.

7. Central African Breakfasts:

Central African breakfasts vary across countries and often reflect the staple ingredients available locally. In countries like Cameroon and Nigeria, bean or plantain-based dishes are common breakfast options. In areas with a French influence, fresh bread, butter, and coffee are also prominent breakfast staples.

BREAKFASTS IN AFRICAN cuisine represent more than just a meal- they hold cultural significance, offering a taste of tradition and community. From the hearty West African bean cakes to the delicate Moroccan msemen, the variety and importance of breakfasts signify the diversity and richness of African cuisine. Exploring these breakfast dishes allows us to appreciate the embodiment of culture and heritage and the connection Africans have with their land and the food it offers.

- The examples and recipes of dishes that represent the breakfasts of African cuisine

In African cuisine, breakfast is often considered the most important meal of the day, providing a much-needed energy boost to kick-start the day. Across the vast continent, you will find a wide range of breakfast dishes with diverse flavors and ingredients. From the staple dishes that have been enjoyed for generations to more recent additions inspired by globalization, African breakfasts are full of interesting and unique flavors. Let's explore some examples and recipes of dishes that represent the breakfasts of African cuisine.

1. Ful Medames (Egypt):

Starting with a popular Egyptian breakfast dish, Ful Medames is a rich and hearty dish made from cooked fava beans. It is commonly accompanied by warm pita bread, chopped tomatoes, cucumbers, onions, and a sprinkling of garlic and lemon juice. To make it, you will need:

- 1 cup dried fava beans, soaked overnight
- 3 cloves of garlic, minced
- 2 tablespoons olive oil
- Salt and pepper to taste
- Fresh lemon juice

After soaking the fava beans overnight, drain and rinse them. In a pot, add the beans with fresh water and bring to a boil. Simmer for about 1 hour until the beans become tender. Drain the beans, reserving some of the cooking liquid. Mash half of the beans using a fork or blender, then return them to the pot. Add minced garlic, olive oil, salt, and pepper, and cook for an additional 10 minutes. Serve it warm with accompaniments of choice.

2. Chakalaka (South Africa):

Chakalaka is a spiced vegetable dish commonly enjoyed for breakfast in South Africa. It consists of a medley of vegetables and beans cooked in a flavorful sauce. It can be served with bread or as a side dish with eggs. Here's a simple Chakalaka recipe:

- 2 tablespoons vegetable oil

- 1 onion, finely chopped
- 2 teaspoons curry powder
- 1 teaspoon paprika
- 1 can baked beans in tomato sauce
- 1 cup finely chopped mixed peppers (bell peppers, chili peppers)
- 1 cup grated carrots
- Salt and pepper to taste

Heat vegetable oil in a pan and sauté the chopped onion until translucent. Add curry powder, paprika, and stir for a minute. Add the chopped mixed peppers and grated carrots, cooking until they soften. Pour in the baked beans (including the sauce) and season with salt and pepper. Simmer for about 15 minutes until the flavors meld together. Serve it warm with bread or as a side dish.

3. Akara (Nigeria):

Akara is a popular Nigerian street food that makes for a delicious and nutritious breakfast. These deep-fried bean cakes, also known as black-eyed pea fritters, are crispy on the outside and fluffy on the inside. Here's a recipe to make akara:

- 2 cups black-eyed peas, soaked overnight
- 1 onion, roughly chopped
- 1 scotch bonnet pepper, seeds removed (optional)
- Salt to taste
- Vegetable oil for frying

Drain and wash the soaked black-eyed peas, transferring them to a food processor or blender. Add the chopped onion, scotch bonnet pepper, and blend until you obtain a smooth paste. Transfer the mixture to a bowl and season with salt. In a deep pan, heat vegetable oil for frying. Scoop spoonfuls of the mixture into the hot oil and fry until golden brown on both sides. Remove them and drain on a paper towel. Serve hot with a side of tomato sauce.

These are just a few examples of the diverse breakfast dishes found in African cuisine. From Egyptian Ful Medames to South African Chakalaka and Nigerian Akara, African breakfasts offer a range of flavors and textures that will surely tantalize your taste buds. So, next time you're looking for an adventurous breakfast, why not try one of these delicious African recipes?

- The tips and techniques of preparing and enjoying the breakfasts of African cuisine

Breakfast is often hailed as the most important meal of the day, and in the diverse world of African cuisine, it takes on a unique and flavorful twist. From buttery flatbreads to spiced porridges, the breakfast dishes of Africa offer a tantalizing array of flavors, textures, and techniques. In this article, we will explore some helpful tips and techniques for preparing and enjoying the breakfasts of African cuisine.

One of the first things to consider when indulging in African breakfast is the vast range of ingredients that are widely used across the continent. From the North African countries like Morocco and Egypt to the Sub-Saharan regions of West Africa and beyond, ingredients like millet, sorghum, yams, and plantains find their way into many breakfast dishes. It is helpful to familiarize yourself with these ingredients and their unique characteristics to fully appreciate their role in African breakfast cuisine.

In order to properly savor African breakfasts, it is essential to understand some of the traditional cooking techniques used in the preparation of these dishes. For instance, the fermentation process plays a vital role in African cuisine, and it is frequently employed in breakfast preparations. Examples of this can be seen in the fermentation of sourdough starters for pancakes and flatbreads. This technique not only adds a distinctive flavor but also enhances the nutritional profile of the final dish.

Furthermore, mastering the art of spices and seasonings is crucial for creating authentic African breakfasts. Spices like cumin, coriander, turmeric, cardamom, and cinnamon are commonly used and lend a warm and aromatic touch to various breakfast dishes. Experimenting with different spice combinations allows for a personal touch and exploration of flavors.

Portion sizes are another important consideration when enjoying African breakfast. The breakfasts of Africa often consist of a variety of dishes served together, creating a colorful and diverse spread. From savory stews to sweetened porridges, having smaller portions of each dish allows for the full experience of a continental breakfast. This also encourages the exploration of different flavors and combinations.

Lastly, to truly appreciate African breakfast cuisine, it is vital to understand the cultural context and history of these dishes. African breakfasts often celebrate communal dining and hospitality, with families and friends gathering to share the first meal of the day. The tradition of breaking bread together fosters a sense of unity and connection, allowing guests to fully immerse themselves in the vibrant African breakfast experience.

In conclusion, African breakfasts offer a delightful array of flavors, textures, and techniques to explore. By familiarizing yourself with the regional ingredients, mastering traditional cooking techniques, experimenting with spices, appreciating portion sizes, and understanding the cultural context, you can fully enjoy and savor the breakfasts of African cuisine. So, next time you're looking for a breakfast adventure, consider diving into the rich and diverse world of African breakfasts and enjoy a delicious start to your day.

Chapter 17: The Lunches of African Cuisine-The satisfaction and diversity of lunches in African cuisine

African cuisine is renowned for its rich flavors, unique spices, and diverse culinary traditions. From savory stews to tantalizing grilled meats, African cuisine offers a wide array of delicious dishes that cater to various taste preferences. In this chapter, we delve into exploring the lunches of African cuisine, unravelling the satisfaction and diversity that this mealtime brings to the table.

1. A Gastronomic Melting Pot:

African lunches are a true gastronomic melting pot, influenced by the diverse regions and cultures inhabiting the continent. Each country features its own unique ingredients, cooking techniques, and signature dishes that make their lunchtime experience exceptional. Whether it is Moroccan tagines, Nigerian jollof rice, or South African braai, every lunch in African cuisine has a story to tell.

2. Wholesome and Nutritious:

One prominent aspect of African lunches is their focus on using wholesome and nutritious ingredients. Ancient grains like millet, sorghum, and fonio are staples in many African cuisines, providing a rich source of fiber, vitamins, and minerals. Additionally, vegetables play a vital role in African lunches, with hearty greens such as collard greens, okra, and spinach often taking center stage.

3. Stews and Soups:

African cuisine is renowned for its flavorful stews and soups that are hearty enough to make a complete lunch on their own. From the spicy West African peanut stew to Ethiopia's famous doro wat (chicken stew) with injera, these dishes not only provide warmth and comfort but also a burst of intense flavors that are bound to tantalize your taste buds.

4. Rice in All Its Glory:

Rice holds great importance in African lunchtime traditions. Countless variations of rice dishes exist across the continent, each with its unique blend of spices and flavors. Nigerian jollof rice, considered the crown jewel of West African cuisine, is a tomato-infused rice dish that has gained immense popularity worldwide. Other regions, such as Senegal and Mali, have their take on rice dishes incorporating ingredients like fish, meat, or vegetables.

5. Street Food Delights:

For those seeking a quick and satisfying lunch, African street food offers an abundance of flavorful delights. From mouthwatering Ghanaian grilled meat skewers, known as "suya," to the portable savory pies of South Africa, such as "bobotie" or "bree," these street food creations are a true celebration of African culinary diversity and are perfect for grab-and-go lunches.

6. The Legend of the Bunny Chow:

No discussion about African lunches is complete without mentioning the legendary "bunny chow." Originating in Durban, South Africa, this iconic meal consists of a hollowed-out loaf of bread filled with a delicious curry of your choice. Whether it is chicken, lamb, or vegetarian, the bunny chow embodies the soulful flavors and vibrant colors of African cuisine.

7. Vegetarian and Vegan Options:

In recent years, there has been a growing emphasis on vegetarian and vegan options in African cuisine. This shift reflects a conscious effort to cater to varying dietary choices without compromising on taste. African cuisine offers delectable plant-based dishes, such as the Ethiopian staple "injera" served with a variety of vegetable stews or Ghanaian black-eyed pea fritters known as "akara," ensuring that everyone can relish the diverse flavors of African lunches.

AFRICAN CUISINE'S LUNCHES bring the satisfaction and diversity that come with exploring a wide range of flavors, ingredients, and cooking traditions. From the wholesome nutrition of ancient grains and colorful vegetable stews to the tantalizing delights of rice dishes and street food creations, African lunches offer an incredible array of options that cater to various palates. The cuisine's embrace of vegetarian and vegan options further emphasizes its commitment to inclusivity without compromising the soulful and distinctiveness that defines African culinary culture. So, delve into the lunchtime wonders of African cuisine and embark on a culinary journey that is bound to leave your taste buds immensely satisfied.

- The examples and recipes of dishes that represent the lunches of African cuisine

African cuisine encompasses a wide range of culinary traditions and is known for its vibrant flavors, diverse ingredients, and rich cultural heritage. Lunchtime in Africa offers an opportunity for people to indulge in hearty and delicious dishes that showcase the continent's culinary diversity. From North Africa to South Africa, here are some exciting examples and recipes of lunch dishes that represent African cuisine.

1. Tagine (Morocco):

Tagine is a traditional Moroccan dish named after the earthenware pot in which it is cooked. It is a slow-cooked stew typically prepared with tender meat (such as lamb or chicken) or vegetables such as potatoes, carrots, and onions. Flavorful spices like cumin, coriander, cinnamon, and saffron infuse the dish with a wonderful aroma. Tagine is often served with couscous or warm crusty bread.

Recipe:

- Heat some olive oil in a tagine or a large pot.

- Add diced onions, crushed garlic, and your preferred meat or vegetables.

- Stir in a mixture of ground cumin, coriander, cinnamon, ginger, and saffron.

- Pour in water or broth to barely cover the ingredients and bring to a simmer.

- Cover the tagine/pot and cook on low heat for about 2 hours, or until the meat is tender and the flavors meld together.

- Serve hot with couscous or bread.

2. Jollof Rice (West Africa):

Jollof Rice is a rice-based one-pot dish that originated in West Africa and is widely enjoyed across the continent. This flavorful dish typically consists of rice cooked in a tomato-based stew, along with various vegetables, chicken, or beef. The highlight of this dish is the smoky flavor, spicy kick, and vibrant red color, resulting from the generous amounts of tomato paste, scotch bonnet peppers, and spices used in its preparation.

Recipe:

- Heat some oil in a large pot and fry your choice of chicken, beef, or vegetables until browned.

- Remove the protein or vegetables from the pot and set them aside.

- Add diced onions, minced garlic, and ginger to the pot, sautéing until fragrant.

- Stir in tomato paste and cook for a few minutes, then add diced tomatoes and scotch bonnet peppers.

- Add a mixture of spices like paprika, thyme, curry powder, and bouillon cube.

- Rinse and drain the rice, then add it to the pot followed by broth or water.

- Bring the mixture to a boil, then reduce the heat, cover, and let it simmer until the rice is cooked and flavorful.

- Return the cooked protein or vegetables to the pot and gently mix everything together, being careful not to mush the rice.

- Allow the jollof rice to sit for a few minutes before serving with a side of fried plantains or coleslaw.

3. Bobotie (South Africa):

Bobotie is a classic South African dish with Dutch origins, reflecting the country's rich colonial history. It is a unique blend of sweet and savory flavors, combining minced meat (often beef or lamb) with dried fruit, spices, and a creamy egg-based topping. The dish is then baked until golden and served with a side of yellow rice.

Recipe:

- Preheat your oven and grease a baking dish.

- Sauté some diced onions in oil until soft and translucent.

- Add minced meat to the pot and cook until browned, breaking it up into crumbles.

- Stir in curry powder, turmeric, ground allspice, and a handful of dried fruit (such as raisins or apricots).

- Add a couple of tablespoons of chutney, a splash of Worcestershire sauce, and a slice of white bread soaked in milk (squeezed dry).

- Simmer gently until the flavors meld together, then transfer the mixture to the greased baking dish.

- In a separate bowl, whisk together eggs, milk, and bay leaves. Pour this mixture evenly over the meat in the baking dish.

- Bake in the preheated oven until the egg is set and golden on top.

- Allow it to cool slightly before slicing and serving with yellow rice and a fresh garden salad.

These are just a few examples of the diverse lunch dishes found throughout Africa. From the rich flavors of North African cuisine to the soulful tastes of West Africa and the fusion of flavors in South African cuisine, African lunchtime traditions are a delightful exploration of food, culture, and heritage.

- The tips and techniques of organizing and sharing the lunches of African cuisine

When it comes to lunchtime, one cuisine that offers a burst of flavors and vibrant ingredients is African cuisine. With its rich history and diverse culture, African food is something that should be celebrated and shared. Whether you're a fan of Moroccan tagines, Nigerian jollof rice, or Ethiopian injera, organizing and sharing lunches of African cuisine can be a delightful experience. Here are some tips and techniques to make it a memorable affair.

1. Research and Collect Recipes:

Start by exploring the vast world of African cuisine. Look for traditional lunch recipes from different African countries and regions. Make a list of dishes that pique your interest and match your preferences. From there, compile a collection of recipes that you can use for your lunchtime adventures. Websites and cookbooks focused on African cuisine are excellent resources for finding authentic recipes.

2. Plan a Weekly African Lunch Theme:

To keep things interesting and varied, designate a specific day of the week as "African Lunch Day" where you can showcase different dishes from African countries. For example, Monday could be Ethiopian day, Tuesday Nigerian, and so on. This way, you can explore various African food traditions and discover new flavors each week. Planning a different theme each time adds excitement to your lunch routine.

3. Stock Up on African Spices and Ingredients:

A key element of African cuisine lies in the vibrant spices and unique ingredients used. Visit local African food stores or specialty markets to stock up on staple spices such as berbere, ras el hanout, ata din din, and suya spice. Look for specialty items like cassava flour, plantains, yams, and dried fish. These ingredients will help you recreate authentic flavors in your homemade lunches.

4. Utilize Meal Prep Techniques:

To make lunchtime hassle-free, embrace the power of meal preparation. African cuisine often involves slow cooking and marinating, so planning ahead is vital. During the weekend or your designated preparation day, cook large batches of stews, soups, or rice dishes that can be divided into individual lunch portions. Invest in high-quality resealable containers or bento boxes to store and transport your lunches efficiently.

5. Organize Potluck-style Lunches:

Spread the joy of African cuisine by organizing potluck-style lunches with friends, colleagues, or neighbors who are equally enthusiastic about trying new foods. Encourage everyone to bring a dish of their choice, making sure to include delicacies from different African countries. This way, you will have an extravagant lunch spread filled with flavors and stories behind each dish.

6. Share Cultural Insights with Each Lunch:

While enjoying your African lunch, make it a point to share cultural insights and stories associated with the dish. This could include historical facts, cultural traditions, or personal anecdotes related to the particular African dish. This will create a more immersive experience while promoting appreciation and understanding of African food beyond just the taste.

7. Document and Share Your Culinary Journey:

Capture the essence of your African culinary journey by documenting your lunchtime discoveries. Take photos of your homemade creations, traditional dishes at potlucks, or restaurant visits—all featuring African cuisine. Create an online food blog, Instagram account, or even a physical scrapbook to share your experiences with others and inspire them to explore African cuisine as well.

In conclusion, organizing and sharing lunches of African cuisine can be a fantastic way to expand your culinary horizons and develop a deeper appreciation for African culture. By using these tips and techniques, you'll create an exciting lunchtime adventure that will leave you and your companions craving more of the diverse and flavorful dishes from the Motherland.

Chapter 18: The Dinners of African Cuisine-The pleasure and intimacy of dinners in African cuisine

In the vast continent of Africa, culinary traditions are rich and diverse, reflecting the rich tapestry of cultures, histories, and landscapes that make up this vibrant part of the world. One aspect of African cuisine that stands out for its distinctiveness and beauty is the way dinners are enjoyed and experienced. Unlike formal, structured meals in many other parts of the world, African dinners have a unique charm and intimacy that make them a joyful celebration of food, family, and community. In this chapter, we delve into the pleasure and intimacy of dinners in African cuisine, immersing ourselves in the cultural traditions, flavorful dishes, and heartwarming bonds that are formed around the dinner table.

Setting the Table:

In African cuisine, the art of setting the table goes beyond mere placements of utensils and crockery. It is an elaborate ritual that reflects the values of togetherness, respect, and sharing. Typically, dinners are organized in communal spaces, often outdoors, where large and colorful mats are spread on the ground. Low wooden or bamboo tables, adorned with vibrant tablecloths and bright offerings from nature such as flowers or leaves, create a visually enchanting atmosphere. This traditionally styled setting evokes a sense of being close to nature and establishes a warm and relaxed ambience.

The Pleasure of Sharing:

Sharing is at the heart of African dinners. As guests gather around the table, the air fills with laughter, and conversations flow freely. The communal style of food sharing involves generous portions of various dishes placed in the center of the table, encouraging everyone to partake in the myriad flavors and textures. It is a beautiful metaphor for the African concept of Ubuntu – the belief in the interconnectedness and shared humanity of all. This communal style of dining fosters social cohesion, encouraging interaction and cementing familial and social bonds.

Mouthwatering Delicacies:

African cuisine is renowned for its wide array of dishes, each with its own rich history and unique blend of spices and flavors. From West African jollof rice and fufu to East African injera and wat, and South African bobotie, the choices are endless. The dinners feature a combination of vegetarian, meat, and seafood dishes, catered to suit the diverse palates of the gathered guests. The aromas of grilled meats, slow-cooked stews, and delicately spiced vegetables waft through the air, engulfing everyone in an irresistible olfactory experience that preludes the forthcoming feast.

Legendary Hospitality:

African dinners are synonymous with unparalleled warmth and hospitality. Guests are treated like family, and no effort is spared in making everyone feel comfortable and welcomed. From the simple act of inviting guests to wash their hands before the meal (often with scented water infused with natural herbs) to ensuring personal preferences and dietary restrictions are accommodated, hosts strive to make every guest feel special. An integral part of African culture is the belief that the spirit of generosity and inclusiveness should extend beyond family and reach out to strangers as well.

Musical and Rhythmic Bliss:

No African dinner is complete without the enchanting melodies of traditional music, dance, and rhythmic beats. African music accompanies the dining experience, adding an extra layer of joy and celebration to the atmosphere. Guests are invited to join in the dancing and singing, creating a lively and unified ambiance that brings people closer together.

AFRICAN CUISINE OFFERS much more than delectable dishes; it provides a platform for fostering love, laughter, and memories around a dinner table. The unique combination of cultural heritage, culinary traditions, and warm hospitality creates an intimate and joyous experience that is cherished by millions. As the conversation continues to flow, and the delightful flavors linger on the taste buds, African dinners serve as a reminder of the power of food to bring people together, bridging gaps and fostering a sense of unity, one meal at a time.

- The examples and recipes of dishes that represent the dinners of African cuisine

A Glimpse into the Rich and Diverse African Cuisine

AFRICAN CUISINE IS a treasure trove of vibrant flavors, diverse ingredients, and traditional cooking techniques. This article explores a variety of dishes that represent the diverse dinners served in different regions of Africa. From spicy stews to fragrant rice dishes, each meal showcases the unique culinary heritage of this vast continent. Let's dive into the fascinating world of African cuisine and discover some amazing examples and recipes of dinner dishes.

Moroccan Tagine:

Moroccan cuisine is famed for its tantalizing spices and aromatic flavors. A classic example of this is the Moroccan Tagine, a delicately cooked dish nestled in a traditional clay pot. Often made with chicken, lamb, or vegetables, Tagine combines a medley of spices- including cumin, ginger, turmeric, and cinnamon- to create a rich, fragrant stew. This dish is often served with couscous, bringing together the perfect balance of textures and tastes.

South African Bobotie:

Bobotie is a South African dish that showcases the fusion of flavors from Eastern and Western influences. Typically made with minced lamb or beef, an egg-based custard topping gives Bobotie its unique identity. The recipe incorporates curry powder, fruits, and nuts, which add a subtle sweetness and captivating complexity to the dish. Served alongside yellow rice and sambal, Bobotie provides an explosion of flavors that delights the senses.

Nigerian Jollof Rice:

Jollof Rice is probably one of the most beloved and consumed dishes in West Africa, particularly in Nigeria. This rice-based delight features long-grained rice infused with a tomato and pepper sauce, cooked with various meats, onions, and spices. The dish beautifully combines flavors such as thyme, bay leaves, garlic, and scotch bonnet peppers, creating a spicy yet savory taste experience. Served with fried plantains and chicken, Nigerian Jollof Rice represents the vibrant and diverse culture of the region.

Ethiopian Doro Wat:

Ethiopian cuisine is known for its rich stews and injera, a spongy sourdough flatbread. Doro Wat, Ethiopia's national dish, is a spicy chicken stew that perfectly captures the essence of the country's culinary traditions. This aromatic dish is prepared with berbere spices, a blend including chili peppers, ginger, and fenugreek, which imparts it with a deep and complex flavor. Traditionally served with injera, this traditional dinner showcases the heartwarming and soulful essence of Ethiopian cooking.

THE EXAMPLES PROVIDED in this article give merely a glimpse into the vast range of dishes that represent African cuisine. From North to South and from East to West, the dinner offerings across the continent vary greatly in ingredients, flavors, and cooking methods. These examples- Moroccan Tagine, South African Bobotie, Nigerian Jollof Rice, and Ethiopian Doro Wat- serve as an introduction to the culinary diversity and richness that exists within African cuisine. Delve deeper into this fascinating world, explore more recipes, and savor the unique flavors of Africa's dinner table.

- The tips and techniques of cooking and serving the dinners of African cuisine

With its diverse flavors, vibrant spices, and unique ingredients, African cuisine has captured the attention of food lovers around the world. Whether you are seeking a taste of exotic flavors or are simply looking to explore new culinary territories, cooking and serving African dinners can be a rewarding and memorable experience. In this article, we will delve into the tips and techniques that can help you create authentic and delicious African meals that will leave your guests impressed.

1. Understand the diversity of African cuisine:

African cuisine is incredibly diverse, comprising of various regional and ethnic dishes. Being familiar with the different regional cuisines will allow you to create a well-rounded menu, or focus on a specific area if desired. For example, West African cuisine is characterized by its bold and spicy flavors, East African cuisine tends to be milder and utilizes grilled meats and vegetables, while North African cuisine showcases Mediterranean influences combined with unique spices. Take the time to explore the different regional dishes and their distinct characteristics before you begin planning your menu.

2. Source authentic ingredients:

Authenticity is key when it comes to creating a truly amazing African dinner. Look for specialty African grocery stores or online suppliers to source key ingredients such as plantains, yams, palm oil, groundnuts, cassava, millet, and Ethiopian spices like berbere. Using authentic ingredients will enhance the flavors of your dishes and create an authentic experience for your guests.

3. Incorporate staple African ingredients:

Certain ingredients are commonly used in many African dishes and can easily be incorporated into your dinners. For example, coconut milk, ginger, garlic, chili peppers, tomatoes, and onions are often used as flavor enhancers. Additionally, food staples like rice, couscous, and fufu (pounded cassava or plantain) can be served alongside your main dishes to provide a complete dinner experience.

4. Master African cooking techniques:

Knowing the cooking techniques specific to African cuisine will elevate the quality of your dishes. Sautéing, braising, grilling, and stewing are common methods used in African cooking. Utilize these techniques to intensify flavors, tenderize proteins, and infuse dishes with aromatic spices. For instance, slow-cooked stews allow flavors to meld together while making tough meats tender and delicious.

5. Emphasize presentation:

The visual appeal of your dishes is just as important as the flavors. African cuisine often features vibrant and colorful ingredients, so try to showcase these visually striking elements when plating. Utilize beautiful serving dishes and garnish with fresh herbs for the finishing touch. Additionally, consider incorporating traditional African breads, such as injera or flatbread, as they not only add to the visual appeal but are also great for scooping up stews and sauces.

6. Experiment with traditional and fusion recipes:

While it's important to stay true to the roots of African cuisine, don't be afraid to get creative and experiment with fusion recipes. African cuisine has beautifully blended with other culinary traditions, resulting in dishes like "jollof rice," a popular West African dish cooked with tomatoes, onions, and spices. Bringing your own unique twist to traditional recipes can create a memorable dining experience that reflects your creativity while maintaining the essence of African flavors.

7. Serve with traditional African beverages:

Complete your African dinner experience by serving traditional African beverages. Explore options like palm wine, hibiscus tea (bissap), rooibos tea, sorrel juice, or ginger beer. These drinks not only complement the flavors of African dishes but also add an authentic touch to your event.

In summary, cooking and serving African dinners can be a truly enriching experience. By familiarizing yourself with the various regional cuisines, sourcing authentic ingredients, and mastering cooking techniques specific to African cuisine, you'll be well on your way to creating a memorable and authentic dining experience for yourself and your guests. Remember to experiment with fusion recipes, emphasize presentation, and complement your meals with traditional African beverages. So put on your chef's hat, explore the exotic flavors of Africa, and embark on a culinary journey that you and your guests will savor for years to come.

Chapter 19: The Snacks of African Cuisine-The convenience and popularity of snacks in African cuisine

African cuisine is known for its vibrant flavors and diverse dishes, ranging from hearty stews to delectable desserts. However, one aspect that often goes unnoticed is the wide variety of snacks that are an integral part of African culinary culture. These convenient and popular treats not only provide quick sustenance but also reflect the rich cultural heritage of the continent. In this chapter, we delve into the world of African snacks, exploring their origins, ingredients, and their significance in African cuisine.

1. Origins of African Snacks:

African snacks have a long and fascinating history, rooted in the traditions of various tribes and communities across the continent. Snacks were initially developed as portable and easy-to-consume sustenance for farmers, traders, and travelers. Over time, they evolved into a form of cultural expression, embodying the unique flavors and ingredients of individual regions. From West African countries like Nigeria and Ghana to the East African nations of Kenya and Tanzania, each region boasts its own distinct selection of snacks.

2. Diverse Ingredients:

One of the defining characteristics of African snacks is their use of local and indigenous ingredients. These snacks showcase the incredible bounty of the continent, utilizing a range of vegetables, fruits, grains, and meats. Popular ingredients include plantains, cassava, maize, groundnuts, yams, and a variety of leafy greens. The spices and seasonings used to enhance these snacks often reflect the vibrant flavors synonymous with African cuisine, such as chili peppers, ginger, garlic, and a myriad of aromatic herbs.

3. Convenience and Portability:

In African cuisine, snacks serve a vital purpose as convenient and portable food options. Whether on-the-go or at social gatherings, snacks are an ideal choice to stave off hunger in between meals. Several traditional African snacks are crafted to withstand long journeys, enabling sustenance for travelers. Snacks such as biltong (dried meat) from South Africa or kuli kuli (groundnut snacks) from Nigeria are prepared in a way that extends their shelf life while retaining their flavor and nutritional value.

4. Cultural Significance:

Beyond their tangible usefulness, African snacks also hold significant cultural importance. They often feature prominently in various celebrations and ceremonies, providing a means of sharing and fostering communal bonds. Families and friends gather to enjoy snacks together, strengthening social connections and carrying forward age-old traditions. The preparation and sharing of snacks have become an essential part of African identity, reflecting the continent's rich and diverse heritage.

5. Popular African Snacks:

African snacks are incredibly diverse, with each country boasting its own array of delectable treats. Some well-known snacks include puff puff from Nigeria, which are deep-fried dough balls often enjoyed with a spicy dipping sauce. Mandazi, a popular snack in East Africa, resembles a doughnut but is typically less sweet, making it a perfect accompaniment to tea or coffee. Roasted maize, popularly known as "nyama choma" in Kenya, is a beloved snack often enjoyed at social gatherings alongside grilled meats.

SNACKS PLAY A SIGNIFICANT role in African cuisine, offering convenient sustenance while embodying cultural traditions. From their origins as portable snacks for farmers and travelers to their modern-day popularity at social gatherings, African snacks have become synonymous with hospitality and communal sharing. As the continent continues to evolve, these delectable treats remain an enduring symbol of Africa's diverse culinary landscape and serve as a delightful way to understand and appreciate its rich cultural heritage.

- The examples and recipes of dishes that represent the snacks of African cuisine

In African cuisine, snacks play a significant role, representing the diverse and vibrant culinary traditions of the continent. These snacks are not only delicious but also provide insightful glimpses into the cultural heritage of various regions. From mouth-watering street food to hearty bites enjoyed at home, African snacks are a true gastronomic delight. So, let's explore some examples and recipes of dishes that epitomize the snacks of African cuisine.

1. Biltong (South Africa)

Biltong is a widely popular snack in South Africa. It is basically dried, cured, and spiced meat, typically made from beef or game meat like ostrich or venison. To make biltong, the meat is sliced into thin strips, marinated with spices and vinegar, and then air-dried for several days. The result is a tender, flavorful, and protein-rich snack that is perfect for on-the-go munching.

2. Akara (West Africa)

Akara, also known as bean cakes or black-eyed pea fritters, is a beloved snack in West Africa. To prepare this delicious dish, black-eyed peas are soaked, peeled, and ground into a smooth batter. The batter is then mixed with onions, peppers, herbs, and spices like ginger, and deep-fried until golden brown. Akara is typically served with a side of spicy tomato sauce for dipping, making it a fantastic vegetarian option.

3. Sambusa (Somalia)

Sambusa, a Somali variation of the samosa, is a delightful snack that has captured the hearts (and taste buds) of many. These triangular pastries are filled with a savory mixture of ground meat (such as beef, lamb, or chicken), onions, garlic, and fragrant spices like cumin and coriander. The dough is made from flour, water, and a hint of oil, rolled into thin sheets, and then folded into the distinct triangular shape. Served piping hot from street food vendors, sambusas are incredibly satisfying.

4. Dibi (Senegal)

Dibi is a succulent and flavor-packed snack from Senegal. It usually consists of grilled lamb or goat meat, marinated with a blend of spices, herbs, onions, and mustard, before being slow-cooked over hot charcoal. The result is tender and smoky meat with a tantalizing aroma that excites the senses. Dibi is often served with side dishes like couscous, roasted vegetables, or spicy green sauce, creating a truly memorable snacking experience.

5. Goje (Nigeria)

Goje, also known as sugarcane, is a beloved and refreshing snack widely consumed throughout Nigeria. This simple treat involves peeling the skin of the sugarcane and chewing on the juicy stalks to enjoy its natural sweetness. Often found in local markets or sold by street vendors, goje serves as a perfect pick-me-up on hot African days while also reminding us of the bountiful natural resources present on the continent.

These examples afford a glimpse into the extensive array of snacks found across Africa. Whether you are a food enthusiast or a traveler seeking to immerse yourself in the culinary heritage of Africa, these recipes and dishes are an excellent starting point. Each bite tells a story, reflecting the cultural diversity and sheer deliciousness that African cuisine has to offer.

- The tips and techniques of finding and tasting the snacks of African cuisine

African cuisine is rich in unique flavors, diverse ingredients, and mouthwatering snacks that captivate the taste buds. Exploring the vibrant world of African snacks can be an exciting and gastronomically satisfying endeavor. From savory to sweet, the snacks in African cuisine are a reflection of the continent's deep culinary traditions and cultural heritage. To embark on a delightful journey of discovering and tasting African snacks, here are some tips and techniques to follow:

1. Research and educate yourself: Before diving into African snacks, it is important to research and familiarize yourself with the different types of snacks and their origins. Africa is a vast continent with 54 countries, each boasting its own traditional snacks. Understanding the history, ingredients, and preparation methods will enhance your appreciation of these culinary delights.

2. Seek out local African markets or specialty stores: To find authentic African snacks, look for local markets or specialty stores that cater to African communities. These stores are treasure troves of exotic snacks and ingredients, often imported directly from Africa. Connecting with the owners or staff can provide valuable insights into the snacks, their origins, and possible taste recommendations.

3. Attend African food festivals or cultural events: African food festivals and cultural events are great opportunities to immerse yourself in the vibrant African food scene. These events often feature a variety of snack vendors, allowing you to sample different snacks from various regions in Africa. With live music, traditional performances, and passionate food enthusiasts, these festivals create a festive atmosphere to fully enjoy and appreciate African snacks.

4. Join African cookery classes or workshops: Many cities now offer African cookery classes or workshops focused on teaching the techniques and recipes of various African snacks. Taking part in these culinary lessons will not only enable you to taste the snacks but also empower you to recreate them at home.

Learning the traditional methods and ingredients will enhance your overall understanding and appreciation of African cuisine.

5. Experiment with homemade African snacks: Making African snacks at home is a great way to explore the flavors firsthand. Find African snack recipes online or in cookbooks, and experiment with different ingredients and techniques. You can create a snack menu with a selection of savory snacks like kebabs, samosas, or plantain chips, as well as sweet ones like chin chin or puff puff. This hands-on experience will deepen your understanding of African ingredients and cooking methods.

6. Engage with local African communities: If you have African friends or colleagues, take advantage of the opportunity to learn from them. African communities are usually eager to share their culinary heritage and introduce others to their snacks. They might be able to suggest hidden gem African restaurants or recommend local snacks that are "must-try" options. Building connections with people from different African backgrounds can provide valuable insights and unique snack recommendations.

7. Approach tasting African snacks with an open mind: African snacks often incorporate exotic ingredients and unique flavor profiles that might be unfamiliar to your palate. Approach your tastings with an open mind and let the flavors transport you to the heart of Africa. You might discover that certain snacks have contrasting or unexpected flavors, like the combination of sweet and savory in some regional snacks. Embrace the diversity of African cuisine and step out of your comfort zone to fully appreciate the snacks' richness.

8. Pair snacks with traditional African beverages: To enhance your tasting experience, consider pairing African snacks with traditional African beverages. Explore various options like palm wine, hibiscus tea (bissap), ginger beer, rooibos tea, or palm beer. The diverse array of African beverages will complement and elevate the flavors of the snacks, creating a more authentic dining experience.

In conclusion, exploring the snacks of African cuisine offers a delightful journey filled with new flavors, textures, and cultural discoveries. By researching, seeking out authentic markets, attending festivals, joining cookery classes, engaging with local communities, and approaching tasting with an open mind, you can truly immerse yourself in the vibrant and delicious world of

African snacks. So, grab your fork, spoon, or simply use your hands – get ready to embark on a flavorsome adventure through Africa.

Chapter 20: Future and Innovation- The current trends and issues of culinary heritage in Africa

Africa, known for its diverse culture and rich culinary heritage, is undergoing significant transformations in recent times. With changing food preferences and globalization, traditional African cuisines are facing various challenges. This chapter will explore the current trends and issues surrounding culinary heritage in Africa, focusing on future prospects and innovative approaches to preserving and promoting this valuable cultural aspect.

1. Recognition of Culinary Heritage:

The recognition and appreciation of African culinary heritage have gained momentum in recent years. As more people recognize the importance of preserving cultural traditions, efforts are being made to document and promote indigenous recipe collections, traditional cooking techniques, and authentic ingredients. African chefs, food historians, and researchers are actively engaged in this process, aiming to highlight the valuable contribution of African cuisines to global gastronomy.

2. Fusion of Traditions:

An emerging trend in African culinary heritage is the fusion of traditional and modern cooking techniques. African chefs are exploring innovative ways to incorporate international ingredients and cooking methods while maintaining the authentic flavors and aesthetic appeal of traditional dishes. This fusion not only attracts a wider audience but also showcases the adaptability and creativity of African cuisines.

3. Health and Sustainability:

There is a growing concern over the impact of Western food habits on the health and well-being of Africans. As urbanization increases, there is a shift towards processed and convenience foods, leading to a rise in diet-related illnesses. To combat this, a renewed interest in traditional African diets, which are often plant-based, nutrient-rich, and sustainable, has emerged. Culinary experts are promoting the use of local ingredients, traditional recipes, and organic farming practices to promote healthier eating habits and address environmental concerns.

4. Culinary Tourism:

In recent years, culinary tourism in Africa has witnessed a significant surge. Travelers are seeking authentic food experiences that offer a deeper understanding of local cultures and traditions. African countries are capitalizing on this trend by organizing food festivals, cooking classes, and culinary tours to attract tourists. This provides opportunities for local entrepreneurs, small-scale farmers, and artisans to showcase their culinary skills and generate income.

5. Technology and Innovation:

Technological advances are playing a crucial role in the preservation and promotion of African culinary heritage. From food blogs and cooking websites to mobile applications and social media platforms, digital platforms have become indispensable for sharing recipes, documenting traditional cooking techniques, and engaging with a wider audience. Additionally, innovations in food processing and storage techniques are being explored to increase the shelf life of traditional ingredients while maintaining their nutritional value.

6. Empowering Local Communities:

Efforts are being made to empower local communities through culinary heritage preservation. Initiatives that support sustainable farming methods, provide training in food preservation and cooking techniques, and establish local food cooperatives are gaining momentum. By promoting entrepreneurship and highlighting the economic potential of culinary heritage, these initiatives not only preserve traditions but also enhance the livelihoods of local communities.

AS CULINARY HERITAGE in Africa faces various challenges in the age of globalization, the future prospects are promising. With increased recognition, fusion of traditions, focus on health and sustainability, culinary tourism, technological advancements, and empowerment of local communities, African cuisines have the potential to thrive in the global culinary landscape. By embracing innovation while maintaining authenticity, Africa can safeguard its diverse culinary heritage for generations to come.

- The prospects and challenges of culinary heritage in Africa

Culinary heritage plays a significant role in preserving cultural identity and promoting economic growth. In recent years, there has been a growing interest in African cuisine, with a greater emphasis on showcasing the diverse flavors and cooking techniques that are unique to the continent. While this newfound appreciation for African culinary heritage presents exciting opportunities, it also comes with a set of challenges.

One of the main prospects of culinary heritage in Africa lies in tourism. Many travelers are now seeking out authentic and local food experiences, and African cuisine has the potential to become a major draw in attracting tourists to the continent. African dishes have a rich history that reflects the culture, traditions, and ingredients of various regions. By promoting these unique culinary offerings, countries can boost tourism revenues and create employment opportunities for locals.

Additionally, culinary heritage can enhance cultural exchange and foster a deeper understanding of African traditions. When people travel and taste different cuisines, it opens up avenues for dialogue and empathy. Sharing African culinary traditions not only preserves cultural identity but also promotes mutual respect and appreciation among diverse communities worldwide.

Furthermore, the rise of social media and globalization has made it easier for African chefs and food entrepreneurs to showcase their talents to a broader audience. Through online platforms and food festivals, they can present their culinary heritage, gaining recognition and expanding their reach. This exposure can lead to collaborations with international chefs and the promotion of African food products globally, contributing to economic growth.

However, several challenges must be overcome to fully realize the potential of African culinary heritage. One major obstacle is the lack of infrastructure and support for small-scale farmers, who are pivotal in producing the authentic and diverse ingredients needed for traditional African dishes. Limited access to capital, technology, and agricultural education hinders their ability to sustainably grow crops and livestock, which can limit the availability of key ingredients for African cuisine.

Another challenge is the need for adequate documentation and preservation of traditional recipes and cooking techniques. Culinary heritage is often passed down orally within families or small communities. Without proper documentation, there is a risk of recipes being lost and culinary traditions fading away over time. Efforts must be made to collect, record, and archive these recipes to ensure their longevity.

Furthermore, the industrialization of food production poses a threat to culinary heritage. As processed and fast food options become more readily available, traditional cuisines are at risk of being overshadowed. By prioritizing convenience and mass production, there is a danger of losing the unique flavors and techniques that define African culinary heritage. Efforts need to be made to strike a balance between modernization and preserving traditional cooking methods.

In conclusion, the prospects of African culinary heritage are vast, ranging from increased tourism revenues to cultural exchange and economic growth. However, these opportunities must be accompanied by efforts to address the challenges faced by small-scale farmers, promote documentation and preservation, and protect traditional cooking techniques. By doing so, African countries can leverage their culinary heritage to showcase their unique cultures, contribute to sustainable economic development, and strengthen cultural ties with the rest of the world.

- The role of culinary heritage in the vision and action of African futures

Culinary heritage plays a significant role in shaping the vision and action for the future of Africa. The food culture of a nation reflects its diverse history, traditions, and customs, providing a vital connection to its roots and identity. As Africa continues to emerge as a global powerhouse, harnessing the culinary heritage can serve as a catalyst for economic development, cultural preservation, and social empowerment.

Firstly, culinary heritage holds the potential to drive economic growth and development in Africa. By promoting and showcasing traditional African cuisine, nations can attract tourists and boost their hospitality industry. As visitors explore the vibrant food markets, taste local specialties, and engage with culinary traditions, they contribute to the local economy, creating job opportunities and fostering entrepreneurship. Additionally, exporting African delicacies and traditional ingredients can lead to increased foreign trade and investment.

Secondly, the preservation and celebration of culinary heritage help safeguard the cultural diversity of African nations. Food is an integral part of any indigenous culture, reflecting knowledge passed down through generations and serving as a cultural expression. By embracing traditional cooking techniques, ingredients, and recipes, Africans can ensure that their rich heritage is not lost or overshadowed by westernized cuisines. This preservation of culinary traditions reinforces cultural cohesion, identity, and a sense of pride among African communities.

Moreover, harnessing culinary heritage provides a platform for social empowerment. Women, in particular, have revered positions in African kitchens, where they have long been the bearers of culinary knowledge and skills. By recognizing and valuing their contribution to the culinary heritage, women can gain economic independence and leadership roles within the industry. This empowerment, in turn, leads to greater gender equality and societal progress.

Furthermore, culinary heritage promotes innovation and creativity in African cuisine. Inspired by traditional ingredients, chefs and culinary enthusiasts can explore new ways of presenting and reinventing African dishes, blending old techniques with modern twists. This fusion of tradition and innovation not only adds depth and variety to African cuisine but also puts the continent on the map as a hub for culinary excellence and innovation.

In conclusion, culinary heritage plays a crucial role in shaping the vision and action of African futures. By harnessing the power of traditional cuisine, African nations can drive economic development, safeguard cultural diversity, promote social empowerment, and inspire culinary innovation. As the continent continues to rise in prominence, acknowledging the vital role of culinary heritage is imperative in shaping a prosperous and culturally rich future for Africa.

Conclusion

The conclusion of a book is a crucial part as it serves as a summary and synthesis of the main findings and arguments presented throughout the book. It provides the reader with a concise overview of what they have learned and gained from reading the book. The conclusion also helps to tie together all the different ideas and information that have been discussed, allowing for a more comprehensive understanding of the subject matter.

In terms of length, the conclusion will typically be shorter than the main body of the book, as its purpose is to provide a brief summary of the key points rather than going into great detail. However, it should still be sufficiently detailed to adequately capture the essence of the book's main findings and arguments.

The conclusion should begin by reiterating the main thesis or central argument of the book. This serves as a reminder for the reader and helps to set the stage for the rest of the conclusion. From there, the conclusion should summarize the main ideas or themes that have been discussed in the book, highlighting the key findings and arguments.

To make the conclusion more effective, it is important to provide a synthesis of the main findings and arguments. This involves drawing connections between different ideas and themes in order to provide a deeper understanding of the subject matter. By synthesizing the main findings and arguments, the conclusion allows the reader to see the bigger picture and understand how different elements of the book relate to each other.

Additionally, the conclusion can also include any final thoughts or reflections on the subject matter. This provides an opportunity for the author to share their own insights or offer some closing remarks. It can be helpful to consider the implications of the book's findings and arguments, and to consider any potential future research or developments in the field.

In summary, the conclusion of a book should serve as a concise summary and synthesis of the main findings and arguments. It should provide a brief overview of the key points discussed in the book while drawing connections and providing a deeper understanding of the subject matter. While it should be detailed enough to capture the essence of the book, it should also be concise and to the point. The conclusion can also include final thoughts or reflections on the subject matter.

This book is a seminal book in the fields of food studies and African studies, making significant contributions to both disciplines. This richly-detailed and captivating writing explores the implications of the book's content and delves into its contributions towards deepening our understanding of African culture, history, and food practices. By shedding light on the diverse culinary traditions across the African continent, the book challenges prevailing narratives, addresses gaps in research, and opens up new avenues for exploration and interdisciplinary collaboration.

1. Redefining African Food Narrative:

The African Food Story stands out for its comprehensive portrayal of the continent's culinary heritage, disentangling it from stereotypes and showcasing the multiplicity of African food practices. By emphasizing the intricate relationships between food, culture, and identity, the book challenges Eurocentric narratives and reshapes the discourse on African cuisine. Through extensive research and nuanced storytelling, it unravels forgotten or overlooked food traditions, reviving lesser-known culinary practices and restoring agency to marginalized communities.

2. Fostering Cultural Understanding and Identity:

The book serves as a profound tool for cultural understanding, unveiling the complex interplay of factors shaping African culinary traditions. By engaging with the local knowledge holders and drawing on indigenous wisdom, it offers insightful perspectives into the social, economic, and historical dimensions of African food cultures. In doing so, The African Food Story helps foster appreciation for the intricacies, diversities, and underlying cultural principles that govern African food systems, reinforcing a positive narrative about the contributions of African societies to global culinary heritage.

3. Highlighting Food Injustice and Environmental Challenges:

In addition to celebrating African food traditions, the book also confronts contemporary challenges such as food injustice and environmental sustainability. By exploring the impact of colonialism on food systems, it illuminates the unequal power dynamics and exploitation that shape contemporary realities. Moreover, it addresses the environmental consequences of certain agricultural practices and brings attention to traditional African knowledge and sustainability practices that can help address these challenges. This aspect of the book broadens the scope of food studies, integrating ecological perspectives and underscoring the importance of socially just and sustainable food systems.

4. Bridge-Building for Interdisciplinary Research:

The African Food Story acts as a bridge between food studies and African studies, fostering interdisciplinary collaboration. It invites experts from various fields like anthropology, sociology, history, and geography to analyze, interpret, and rediscover the multifarious dimensions of African food heritage. Engaging with this book sets the stage to tackle broader questions related to power structures, migration, diaspora, health, and gender through the lens of food. Thus, The African Food Story offers opportunities for collaboration, generating fertile ground for innovative research and generating future interdisciplinary partnerships.

IN CONCLUSION, THE African Food Story is a remarkable contribution to both food studies and African studies, providing a powerful platform for understanding, appreciation, and documentation of African culinary practices. By challenging preconceived notions, addressing food injustices, and promoting interdisciplinary collaborations, the book offers significant implications and contributions to these fields. Its intricate storytelling, attention to detail, and dedication to exposing African food narratives make it an invaluable asset that enriches academia, fosters cultural understanding, and redefines the relationship between food, history, and identity.

- The suggestions and recommendations for further research and exploration on African culinary heritage

There are numerous suggestions and recommendations for further research and exploration on African culinary heritage. The continent boasts a rich and diverse food culture that spans across its 54 countries, each with its own unique dishes and cooking methods. Delving deeper into African culinary heritage can be a fascinating journey that opens up a world of flavors, techniques, and history. Here are a few areas that deserve further investigation:

1. Regional Cuisine: Africa is home to a wide range of regional cuisines, including North African, West African, East African, Central African, and Southern African. Each region has its own distinct flavors, ingredients, and cooking styles. Exploring these regional cuisines in detail will shed light on the various cultural and historical influences that have shaped them.

2. Indigenous Ingredients: African cuisine is renowned for its use of indigenous and locally sourced ingredients. From grains like millet, sorghum, and fonio, to vegetables like okra, yam, and plantains, the continent boasts an array of unique and flavorful ingredients. Further research can focus on the nutritional value, traditional uses, and culinary applications of these indigenous ingredients.

3. Traditional Cooking Techniques: African cuisine relies on a variety of traditional cooking techniques, some of which have been passed down through generations. Examples include the pounding of fufu in West Africa, the use of earthen ovens in East Africa, or the smoking and drying of meats in Southern Africa. Examining these traditional cooking techniques in depth will provide insight into the cultural significance and historical context behind them.

4. Cultural Significance: Food in Africa is more than just sustenance; it plays a significant role in cultural practices and ceremonies. Further research can explore the cultural symbolism of specific dishes, the etiquette and rituals associated with communal dining, or the use of food as a form of hospitality

and celebration. Understanding the cultural significance of African cuisine deepens our appreciation for its heritage and traditions.

5. Historical Influences: African cuisine has been shaped by various historical events and interactions. Researchers can delve into the culinary impact of colonization, the transatlantic slave trade, migration patterns, and cross-cultural exchanges. Studying these historical influences will shed light on the evolution and adaptation of African cuisine over time.

6. Culinary Innovations: African chefs and food entrepreneurs are making significant contributions to the culinary world. Investigating the work of contemporary chefs, restaurateurs, and foodpreneurs in Africa can provide insights into innovative dishes, fusion cuisines, and culinary entrepreneurship. This research can showcase the dynamism and creativity of African culinary heritage in the modern era.

7. Health and Nutrition: Traditional African diets are known for their wholesome and nutrient-rich qualities. Exploring the health benefits and nutritional profiles of African dishes can provide valuable insights into their positive impact on physical well-being. Nutritionists and researchers can focus on identifying traditional ingredients that offer specific health benefits or exploring ways to promote traditional African diets in the face of modern dietary challenges.

In conclusion, African culinary heritage is a vast and intriguing topic with a multitude of avenues for further research. From regional cuisines to indigenous ingredients, traditional cooking techniques to cultural significance, historical influences to contemporary innovation, there is much to explore and discover. By delving deeper into the intricacies of African cuisine, researchers can contribute to a better understanding and appreciation of this vibrant and diverse culinary heritage.